A Little Something

A Little Something

More Than 150 Snacks,
Hors d' Oeuvres, and Appetizers for Every
Craving and Occasion

SUSAN EPSTEIN

William Morrow and Company, Inc.
New York

641.812
EPS

Library of Congress Cataloging-in-Publication Data

Epstein, Susan.
    A little something : more than 150 snacks, hors d'oeuvres, and appetizers for every craving and occasion / Susan Epstein.
        p.   cm.
    Includes index.
    ISBN 0-688-15572-3
    1. Appetizers.   2. Snack foods.   I. Title.
    TX740.E64   1998
    641.8' 12—dc21   98-4705
                                                            CIP

Printed in the United States of America

First Edition

1 2 3 4 5 6 7 8 9 10

BOOK DESIGN BY RENATO STANISIC

www.williammorrow.com

In memory of my mother,
Esty Moskowitz, who was
my dearest friend, my role
model, my cheerleader, and
my inspiration

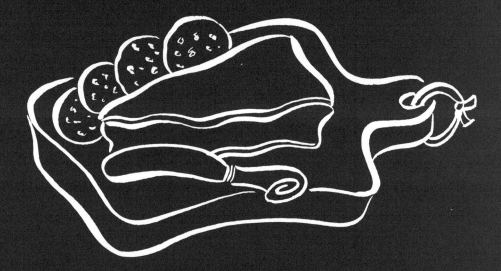

Contents

Introduction

There is no doubt about it. We can call them snacks, hors d'oeuvres, appetizers, dunks, nibbles, or bites. We can indulge in them at parties or while relaxing with family. We can serve them mid-morning or afternoon, after school, at formal cocktail parties, at the weekly poker game, at tea time, during the Super Bowl, or at midnight. We just love to eat them. Every now and then, we need a little something.

These "little somethings" might be in addition to meals or in lieu of them; they might precede meals or follow them. For the cook, they provide creativity and ease; for the eater, adventure and satisfaction in bite-size portions. Even kids will try something that can be consumed in one or two bites.

To prepare a little something for ourselves, family, or close friends, we can use our instincts and cravings as a guide. But, when entertaining, the menu will depend on the type of occasion and guest list, the budget, the time we have to prepare, and how the little somethings will be served.

The Occasion and Guests

Obviously, the menu for a midnight craving, an after-school snack, or an informal card game will be quite different from pre-theater tidbits or cocktails with prospective clients. My simple advice is know your crowd.

I will never forget setting out what I thought was an interesting selection of gourmet tidbits and finding them in the same spot, barely touched, an hour later, while the chips had already been refilled and someone asked if I had some onion soup dip.

Now, I'm certainly not recommending onion soup dip—although it is fun every now and again—but make sure you have "tasters" before you serve a variety of exotic pizzas but no plain tomato and cheese. Serve gourmet food to gourmets and updated traditional tidbits to the less adventurous. Follow this simple advice: Plan an eating adventure, but have one or two "life jackets" on hand just in case. (See You Can't Go Wrong, *page 7.)*

The Budget

Like it or not, most of us have to decide how much money we can spend on this little eating adventure. Again, balance is the key. Temper one or two expensive tidbits with a variety of less costly ones. Remember, elegant does not have to mean expensive (see Elegant on a Budget, *page 7).*

Time

Here's something most of us need more of, no matter what the occasion. To avoid extreme anxiety, an inability to enjoy your guests and food, and a severe case of indigestion, have a plan. Create a menu that can be prepared almost completely in advance (aside from a few last-minute fixes). Decide how far in advance you can make each item and what needs to be made last minute; what needs to be reheated and for how long; what is served cold, and what will need refills. Make a shopping list, but leave time for a last-minute run to the supermarket or bakery. Plan and do as much in advance as possible.

Of course, there are times when planning is just not possible. Sometimes people drop by and stay for awhile. You want to offer them "a little something," but you certainly don't want to spend much time in the kitchen preparing it; you want to enjoy their visit.

This is one of those times when a stocked pantry and freezer will be an invaluable tool. (See The Ready-to-Munch Pantry and Freezer, page 17, for suggestions.)

Serving

The recipes in A Little Something are relatively easy to serve. With large groups, it is easiest to set up a buffet and let guests help themselves. With smaller groups, you have more leeway; you can pass around hors d'oeuvres, set up a buffet, or do both. The question is: How much help will you have? If you are on your own (barring a few good souls who will help you set up), stick with a buffet. You'll have more time to enjoy the guests and the food. If you are hiring kitchen help, the amount of assistance you'll need will depend on the menu you choose.

Creating a Menu

This is when your creativity and cravings take control. The possible combinations are almost endless. You can create menus featuring a particular cuisine, such as Mexican, or particular foods, such as cheese and wine. You can choose comfort foods like nachos or more elegant hors d'oeuvres like stuffed pastry puffs. You can choose foods that fit a theme, such as the Super Bowl, or setting, such as the garden or pool.

The recipes, tips, and menus in A Little Something *will satisfy your urge to munch, crunch, nibble, bite, and dunk at any occasion or no occasion. There is something for everyone—from tomato bruschetta or sesame pecan chicken tenders to pizzas, cookies, or espresso. Each recipe is easy to prepare and quick to make, leaving you plenty of time to savor these tasty tidbits and enjoy your guests. Whether it's a quick pick-me-up, an after-school snack, a poolside nibble, an after-theater treat, a coffee break, a midnight munch, or an elegant hors d'oeuvre platter, you'll find the perfect "something" here.*

So treat yourself. Have a little something now!

Cocktail Party Tidbits

Each of these can be easily eaten while holding a drink.

- Stuffed Mushrooms

- Cocktail Meatballs

- Horseradish Tuna on
  Cucumber Rounds

- Cherry Tomatoes with
  Vegetable Crabmeat Filling

- Fried Won Tons

- Spinach and Feta Puffs

- Sausage in Blankets

- Bacon-wrapped Shrimp

- Smoked Salmon "Flowers"

- Fresh Vegetables Stuffed with
  Scallion, Radish, and Carrot
  Cream Cheese

- Crostini

- Tomato Bruschetta

- Dilled Shrimp Salad on Endive
  Leaves

- Marinated Niçoise Olives

- Marinated Artichokes and
  Mushrooms

- Orange Macadamia Nuts

- Glazed Walnuts

Holiday Nibbles

This is an impressive, elegant menu of nibbles. With the exception of broiling the bacon-wrapped shrimp and baking the Brie, this menu can be done entirely in advance.

- Baked Brie Stuffed with Strawberry Preserves and Toasted Almonds
- Camembert with Apricot Preserves, Pecans, and Dried Cranberries, surrounded by a variety of crackers and dippers
- Breadsticks with Prosciutto and Robiola

- Basil Pesto Dip with Crudités
- Chicken Satay with Thai Peanut Sauce
- Bacon-wrapped Shrimp with Soy Dipping Sauce
- Smoked Salmon "Flowers"
- Glazed Walnuts
- Orange Macadamia Nuts
- Double Peanut Brittle

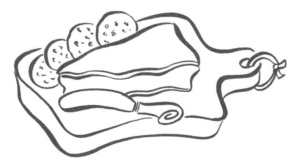

Elegant on a Budget

Here's a menu fit for a king, but it won't break the royal bank!

- Tricolor Tortellini Skewers with Roasted Pepper and Garlic Dip
- Garlic and Herb Tomatoes on Crostini
- Mini Crab Cakes or Potato Pancakes

- Spinach and Feta Puffs or Fried Won Tons
- California Nachos
- Berry Dip and Chocolate Sauce with assorted fruit
- Variety of Brewed Coffee and Espresso Specialties

You Can't Go Wrong

Here's my list of standbys—foods that almost everyone likes. To be safe, I like to include at least one at my gatherings.

- Tomato Bruschetta
- Crostini
- Sesame Pecan Chicken Tenders
- Personal Pizzas
- Assorted vegetable crudités with Garlic Aïoli, Tomato Salsa, or Basil Pesto Dip

- Foccacia in a Snap
- Garlic and Cheese Twists
- Nachos
- Spinach and Feta Puffs
- Stuffed Mushrooms
- Deviled Eggs
- Stuffed Potato Skins

Poolside Hors d'Oeuvres

Here's a menu that fits the summer season—casual, relaxed, with a minimal amount of time needed in the kitchen.

- Pesto, Olive, and Artichoke Pizza
- Zucchini Rolls
- Tomato Bruschetta
- Dilled Shrimp Salad on Endive
  Leaves

- Ice Cream Cookiewiches
- Nutty Thumbprint Cookies
- Island Delights, Sorbet Sodas,
  and Fresh Fruit Spritzers

Tex-Mex Munchies

Here's an easy menu that will spice up any occasion. Have a blender and lots of cold drinks nearby.

- Green Sauce or Black Bean Dip
  with Pita Chips
- Nachos Grandes
- Variety of Quesadillas

- Tex-Mex Hot Dogs
- Southwestern Mix
- Island Delights
- Fresh Fruit Spritzers

A Taste of Italy

This is an excellent menu for cheese lovers. A variety of wine also adds a nice touch.

- Marinated Artichokes and Mushrooms
- Breadsticks with Prosciutto and Robiola
- Marinated Goat Cheese with Crumb Crust
- Crostini topped with Goat Cheese and Sun-dried Tomato and Roasted Pepper Pesto

- Puttanesca Focaccia in a Snap
- Scallops Oreganata
- Plum Tomatoes with Mozzarella and Prosciutto Stuffing
- Chocolate Hazelnut Thins and Lemon Pignoli Crisps
- Variety of Brewed Coffee and Espresso Specialties

Pub Food

This menu will bring baby boomers back to their college days. Have a pitcher of beer close by. A music mix from the late 1970s or early 1980s would also be a nice touch.

- Buffalo Chicken Wings
- Nachos
- Stuffed Potato Skins
- Oven-fried Zucchini with Horseradish Yogurt Sauce
- Crispy Onion Rings with Spicy Dipping Sauce

Super Bowl Snacks

This is a fun menu that needs a minimum amount of kitchen time during the big game. Prepare skins and nachos in advance and simply bake as needed.

- Broccoli and Cheese Bread
- Open-faced Roast Beef sandwiches
- Turkey Cranberry Rollwiches
- Stuffed Potato Skins
- Nachos
- Southwestern Mix
- Caramel Munch
- Ice Cream Cookiewiches
- Lemonade, Flavored Iced Tea, and beer

Midnight Munchies

It's late, but those hunger pangs just won't quit. . . . Here are some great combinations to tide you over until morning. Use decaffeinated coffee and tea; otherwise you may need another snack before morning!

- Tomato Sandwich and Flavored Iced Tea
- Grilled Fontina, Sun-dried Tomato, and Bacon Sandwich and Hot Chocolate
- Turkey Cranberry Rollwich and Flavored Iced Tea
- Pretzel Rolls and Chocolate Peanut Butter Banana Shake

- Open-faced Roast Beef Sandwich and Lemonade
- Gourmet English Muffin and Brewed Coffee Specialty of your choice
- Personal Pizza and Lemonade

Cheese with Preserves, Jams, and Chutneys

Cheese served with fruit and vegetables is a classic combination. And what could be an easier snack or hors d'oeuvre than a thin layer of preserves spread on a cracker and topped with cheese? Sprinkle on some chopped nuts if you like. Here are some of my favorite combinations:

- **Strawberry preserves and Brie**
- **Red pepper jam and goat cheese**
- **Apricot preserves and Brie**
- **Apple butter and cheddar**
- **Raspberry preserves, chopped almonds, and mascarpone**
- **Plum jam and creamy Havarti**
- **Peach jam, chopped pecans, and ricotta**
- **Fig preserves and goat cheese or marscarpone**
- **Mango chutney and cheddar**
- **Guava jelly and cream cheese or creamy ricotta**
- **Apricot preserves and Roquefort**
- **Blackberry or blueberry preserves and Bleu de Bresse**
- **Cranberry chutney or relish, chopped walnuts, and Robiola**
- **Raspberry preserves, chopped pecans, and sweet Gorgonzola**
- **Cherry preserves, chopped cashews, and Brie**
- **Peach chutney and goat cheese**

The Hot Hors d'Oeuvre Party

Here's a fabulous menu for a winter cocktail party by the fire.

- **Stuffed Mushrooms**

- **Spinach and Feta Puffs**

- **Sausage in Blankets**

- **Bacon-wrapped Shrimp with Soy
  Dipping Sauce**

- **Scallops Oreganata**

- **Roasted Pepper Focaccia
  in a Snap**

- **Gingerbread**

- **Strawberries with Chocolate
  Sauce**

The Cold Hors d'Oeuvre Party

Here's an easy menu that requires no heating up. Simply prepare the platters and enjoy your guests.

- Crostini Topped with Sun-dried Tomato and Roasted Pepper Pesto and Goat Cheese
- Assorted crudité platter with Basil Pesto Dip
- Zucchini Rolls
- Horseradish Tuna on Cucumber Rounds
- Dilled Shrimp Salad on Endive Leaves
- Chicken Satay with Thai Peanut Sauce
- Lemon Pignoli Crisps
- Nutty Thumbprint Cookies
- Coffees, Flavored Iced Tea, and Lemonade

Elegant Springtime Treat

- Strawberry Shortcakes
- Chocolate Hazelnut Thins
- Variety of Brewed Coffee and Espresso Specialties

Summer Hors d'Oeuvres in the Garden

- **Mini Crab Cakes with Spicy Dipping Sauce**
- **Pita Pizza**
- **Tricolor Tortellini Skewers with Roasted Pepper and Garlic Dip**
- **Puff Pastry with Smoked Salmon Filling**
- **Basil Pesto Dip with crudités**

Coffee and . . .

For most of us, a good cup of coffee needs a little something to go with it. Here's a list of wonderful combinations—or combine any of the coffees and desserts throughout the book.

- **Cappuccino and Chocolate Hazelnut Thins**
- **Café con Panna and Nutty Thumbprint Cookies**
- **Mochaccino and Chocolate Cookie Bars**
- **Mocha Latte and Raisin Nut Twists**
- **Café Vanilla and Cranberry Orange Scones**
- **Café Latte and Strawberry Shortcakes**
- **Café con Panna and White Chocolate Raisin Nut Bark**
- **Café Mocha and Hazelnut Blondies**
- **Espresso Romano and Lemon Pignoli Crisps**

Teatime

This is an elegant and satisfying menu that will turn the simplest get-together into a special occasion. Perfect when "the red carpet treatment" is needed or when a few good friends get together to catch up.

- Finger Sandwiches
- Lemon Pignoli Crisps
- Hazelnut Blondies
- Nutty Thumbprint Cookies
- Variety of coffees and teas

The Dessert Bar

A menu of sweets that's perfect after the show, when everyone is going back to your house for dessert. Make the Easy Fruit Cobbler the day before—it takes about 40 minutes, baking time included. All the cookies can be made in advance and frozen. The walnuts and bark will keep for a few weeks in airtight containers. Just take the cookies out before you leave and put up a pot of coffee when you get home.

- Chocolate Hazelnut Thins
- Lemon Pignoli Crisps
- Nutty Thumbprint Cookies
- Raisin Nut Twists
- Easy Fruit Cobbler
- Assorted ice creams and sorbets
- Chocolate Truffles with Kahlúa and Pecans
- White Chocolate Raisin Nut Bark
- Variety of Brewed Coffee and Espresso Specialties

The Ready-to-Munch Pantry and Freezer

The doorbell rings. It's 10 A.M. and a few friends have stopped by before a day of shopping at the local flea market . . . It's 3 P.M. and your son arrives home with four of his hungry buddies after a game of touch football . . . It's 9 P.M., and a few couples are going back to your house for a snack after the movie . . . Your lunch guests stayed so long, they are hungry—again . . . It's midnight and you need a little something . . . You want to offer a little something to these drop-in guests (or yourself), but the refrigerator is bare.

By keeping a stocked pantry and freezer, you can whip up a little something in minutes, anytime. Here's a list to help you get started. It includes items you'll need "just in case" and items that should be staples in your "ready-to-munch" pantry or freezer. Make sure you add your favorites and a variety of healthy alternatives. And some of the terrific gourmet foods available in specialty stores—they make wonderful additions to any menu. Of course, even good-quality ready-mades may not be as good as homemade and are usually expensive. But in a pinch, you'll be glad you had a jar or two.

PANTRY STAPLES

- Anchovies
- Assorted chips, popcorn, and pretzels
- Assorted condiments (cocktail sauce, horseradish sauce, tartar sauce, ketchup, barbecue sauce, mayonnaise, duck sauce)
- Assorted crackers
- Assorted dried fruit
- Assorted nuts
- Assorted vinegars (rice, balsamic, red wine, raspberry, etc.)
- Baking chocolate
- Canned beans (black, chick peas, refried, etc.)
- Canned fish and shellfish (tuna, salmon, lump crabmeat, chopped clams)
- Caponata
- Caviar
- Chutney
- Cured sausages and meats
- Dijon mustard
- Flavored oils (garlic, basil, red pepper, oregano, etc.)
- Honey
- Horseradish
- Hot sauce, Tabasco
- Marinated artichokes
- Mexican salsa
- Olive oil
- Olives
- Pâtés
- Pesto sauce
- Pizza sauce

- Roasted peppers
- Rolled oats
- Salad dressings
- Soy sauce
- Sun-dried tomatoes

- Tomato sauce
- Variety of baking chips (milk, white, and dark chocolates, peanut butter, Heath Bar Brickle)

Freezer Staples

- Assorted sorbets, frozen yogurts, or ice creams
- Cocktail pumpernickel, rye
- French bread

- Italian pizza bread shells
- Pita bread
- Refrigerated pizza dough, bread dough, puff pastry dough

Something to Nibble

When chatting with a few close friends, entertaining a crowd, watching a new video, enjoying the weekly card game, or rooting for a favorite team, people love to dip, nibble, munch, and crunch. It's quick, neat, and fun.

These dips, salsas, nibbles, and cheeses are a breeze to prepare, and some have the hidden bonus of being low in fat and calories. Simply set them out with a variety of vegetables, crackers, breads, breadsticks, chips, and pretzels to use as "dippers." Don't forget to make lots of extras—munchies go quickly.

Read package labels carefully when purchasing "dippers"—many are loaded with fat and calories (and let's face it: most of us indulge with generous portions). Experiment with low-fat products; some are so good you can barely taste the difference. Or, if you have the time, make a batch of your own low-fat "dippers."

PITA CHIPS

This delicious newcomer to the chip category provides flavor and crunch when you need to munch. Plus, these chips have very little fat. They are great with any salsa or dip. Make sure you prepare an extra batch—there's always room for another chip.

MAKES 4 SERVINGS

Savory Chips
2 pita breads
Olive oil cooking spray
¼ teaspoon garlic powder
¼ cup freshly grated Parmesan cheese
  (optional)

Sweet Chips
2 pita breads
Butter-flavored cooking spray

1 tablespoon sugar
¼ teaspoon ground cinnamon

Mexican Chips
2 pita breads
Vegetable oil cooking spray
¼ teaspoon cayenne pepper
¼ teaspoon chili powder
¼ teaspoon salt

1. Preheat the oven to 350°F.

2. Using small kitchen scissors or a knife, carefully split each pita round into 2 equal circles along the edge. Cut each circle into 6 wedges.

3. With the cooking spray, evenly cover each wedge on both sides.

4. Combine the remaining ingredients and sprinkle evenly over the wedges.

5. Bake at 350° for 8 to 10 minutes, until golden. Cool completely and serve with dip.

BAGEL CHIPS

Sliced thin and baked, bagels are a crunchy, low-fat snack. Enjoy them on their own, as dippers, or topped with spreads. For an excellent mid-morning snack, spread the chips with some light cream cheese, light peanut butter, or all-fruit spread. This is a great way to use up day-old bagels.

MAKES 12 PIECES

2 bagels of your choice

Vegetable, olive oil, or butter- or garlic-flavored cooking spray

1. Preheat the oven to 350°F.

2. Cut each bagel into at least 6 thin slices, and place them on a baking sheet. Coat with the cooking spray of your choice.

3. Bake about 6 minutes until crisp and golden. Turn the slices over, coat with the spray, and bake an additional 6 minutes. Store in airtight containers.

Bagel chips make excellent hors d'oeuvres when topped with:

- **Sour cream and caviar**
- **Plain or flavored cream cheese**
- **Caponata**
- **Brie and apple slices**
- **Creamy goat cheese and arugula**
- **Fontina and thin tomato slices**
- **Black Olivada (page 39) and Muenster cheese**
- **Smoked Salmon Spread (page 109)**
- **Sun-dried Tomato and Roasted Pepper Pesto (page 85)**

TORTILLA CRISPS

These crispy strips remind me of Chinese noodles, so I like to have a bowl of duck sauce nearby—and lots of refills.

Vegetable oil cooking spray
Six 6-inch flour tortillas, cut into
  ¼-inch strips or small triangles
4 tablespoons olive oil

1 teaspoon garlic powder
2 to 3 tablespoons freshly grated
  Parmesan cheese
Salt to taste

1. Preheat the oven to 350°F. Coat a baking sheet with cooking spray.

2. Place the tortilla strips in a bowl, and add the oil and garlic powder. Toss to coat.

3. Transfer strips in one layer to baking sheet. Sprinkle on the Parmesan cheese and salt.

4. Bake, stirring occasionally, 15 to 20 minutes, until crisp. Cool completely. Store in an airtight container for up to 1 week.

For low-fat Tortilla Crisps, use low-fat flour tortillas. Omit the oils and coat strips with a generous amount of garlic-flavored cooking spray. Sprinkle with salt and bake as directed above.

GARLIC AND CHEESE TWISTS

These look lovely on a buffet table, but you'll also enjoy munching them while watching a good movie.

Vegetable oil cooking spray
2 puff pastry sheets (10 by 15 inches),
  thawed
½ cup milk

2 egg whites
2 teaspoons garlic powder
2 cups freshly grated Parmesan cheese

1. Preheat the oven to 400°F. Coat a baking sheet with cooking spray.

2. Open the puff pastry and lay the sheets flat on a clean surface.

3. In a small bowl, beat the milk and egg whites together. Brush evenly over one side of each pastry sheet.

4. Sprinkle each sheet with ½ teaspoon garlic powder and ½ cup cheese. Roll lightly with a rolling pin to adhere. Turn over and repeat.

5. Using a sharp knife or pizza cutter, cut the pastry into long strips. Twist each strip. Sprinkle evenly with the remaining garlic powder and cheese.

6. Bake about 20 minutes, until golden.

For Cinnamon Twists, omit the garlic powder and cheese. Substitute 1 cup sugar mixed with 2 teaspoons ground cinnamon. After brushing each pastry with the milk and egg mixture, sprinkle each sheet with ¼ cup sugar and ½ teaspoon ground cinnamon. Roll lightly with a rolling pin to adhere. Turn over and repeat. Prepare and bake.

GARLIC KNOTS

A basket of hot knots, a variety of cheeses, cured sausages, and a good bottle of red wine—a superb combination.

Vegetable oil cooking spray
One package refrigerated pizza dough
¼ cup garlic-flavored oil or olive oil
*   mixed with 2 cloves garlic, minced*

Freshly grated Parmesan cheese
(optional)

1. Preheat the oven to 425°F. Spray a baking sheet with the cooking spray.

2. Divide the dough into 20 pieces. Roll each piece into an 8- to 10-inch rope. Tie each rope into a knot and tuck end pieces under roll.

3. Liberally brush each knot with garlic oil. Sprinkle with grated Parmesan if desired.

4. Bake 10 to 13 minutes, until golden. Brush with an additional layer of garlic oil, if desired.

How about Basil Knots or Oregano Knots? Just substitute your favorite flavored oil for the garlic oil.

> Turn stale bread into crunchy breadsticks in minutes: Cut bread into thin strips and brush with a thin coating of flavored oil. Bake at 350°F., 15 to 20 minutes, until crisp.

BLACK BEAN DIP

Packed with flavor and fat free, this delicious dip is great with raw vegetables, tortilla chips, Bagel Chips (page 23) or Pita Chips (page 22). It also adds a zing to quesadillas or Mexican pizza. Just spread on a thin layer and top with your favorite cheese and salsa and cook as directed.

MAKES 2 CUPS

One 19-ounce can black beans,
    drained and rinsed
1 tablespoon chopped red onion
¼ cup chopped red bell pepper
2½ tablespoons cider vinegar
1 to 2 tablespoons finely diced
    jalapeño peppers or jarred pickled
    jalapeño peppers

1 teaspoon chili powder
1 tablespoon chopped fresh cilantro
Salt and freshly ground pepper to taste

Puree all of the ingredients, except the salt and pepper, in the bowl of a food processor. Puree until combined, and add the salt and pepper to taste. Place in a tightly covered plastic container and store in the refrigerator for up to 1 week.

TOMATO SALSA

Once you taste this zesty fresh salsa and see how easy it is to make, you'll take jarred salsa off your shopping list.

MAKES 2 CUPS

8 plum tomatoes, diced
3 tablespoons finely diced red onion
¼ cup canned diced green chili
   peppers, drained

2 tablespoons finely chopped fresh
   cilantro
1 tablespoon fresh lime juice
Salt and freshly ground pepper to taste

Stir all of the ingredients together in a large bowl until blended. Adjust the seasoning to taste. Refrigerate for at least 3 hours to let the flavors blend.

Create your own unique salsas by adding any of the following ingredients:

- **Minced garlic**
- **Chopped cucumber**
- **Chopped red bell pepper**
- **Minced jalapeño pepper**

- **Chopped peaches**
- **Chopped mango**
- **Black beans**

Green Sauce

Chef Raúl Juárez of El Rio Grande in New York City shared his fabulous recipe for green sauce. I know you'll love it as much as I do with tortilla chips and a frozen Island drink (page 164).

(page 164)

MAKES 2 CUPS

5 green tomatoes, blackened
2 green jalapeño peppers, roasted and
    seeded
2 avocados, peeled and pitted

¼ cup chopped fresh cilantro
1 tablespoon garlic powder
5 tablespoons sour cream
2 teaspoons salt

Place all the ingredients in a food processor or blender and puree until smooth. Adjust the seasoning to taste.

To roast peppers, place the peppers on a broiler rack or over a gas flame until the skins are thoroughly blackened. Transfer to a paper bag and tightly close for 15 minutes. The skin will easily slip off using your fingers or a small paring knife.

To blacken green tomatoes, place the tomatoes on a rack of a broiler or over a gas flame until the skin blisters, cracks, and slightly blackens. Let cool slightly and peel off the skin, if desired.

SPICY MANGO SALSA

This unusual salsa makes a good dip for low-fat tortilla chips, pita chips, celery sticks, or endive leaves. Make a little extra for dinner and use it as a topping for grilled fish or fajitas. With the help of a food processor, this salsa comes together in less than 10 minutes.

MAKES 2½ CUPS

1 large, ripe mango or papaya, or
   2 large peaches, peeled, pitted,
   and finely chopped
¼ cup finely chopped red onion
¼ cup finely chopped red bell pepper
1 cup finely chopped seeded tomatoes

4 tablespoons fresh lime juice
1 tablespoon chopped fresh cilantro
1 tablespoon finely chopped jalapeño
   pepper, or to taste
Salt and pepper to taste

Mix all the ingredients together in a medium bowl. Adjust the seasoning to taste. Let stand at least 30 minutes to let the flavors blend.

LIGHT AND CREAMY SALSA DIP

This dip is equally good with chips or a vegetable platter.

1 cup Mexican salsa
½ cup fat-free mayonnaise
¼ cup light or fat-free sour cream

2 tablespoons canned tomato sauce
3 tablespoons water

Combine all the ingredients in a small bowl and stir to combine.

Other interesting and light crudité dips:

- **1 cup plain yogurt and 2 to 3 tablespoons Sun-dried Tomato and Roasted Pepper Pesto (page 85)**

- **1 cup plain yogurt and 2 to 3 tablespoons honey mustard**
- **Roasted Pepper and Garlic Dip (page 99)**

THAI PEANUT SAUCE

Here's something different to serve with raw or steamed vegetables. It also works well as a dip for Chicken Satay. For a spicier version, add a teaspoon or two of curry powder or some curry paste.

½ cup creamy peanut butter
1½ tablespoons soy sauce
1 teaspoon minced fresh ginger
1½ tablespoons fresh lemon juice

1 large clove garlic, minced
¾ teaspoon crushed red pepper flakes
1 teaspoon sugar
½ cup warm water

Place the peanut butter, soy sauce, ginger, lemon juice, garlic, red pepper flakes, and sugar in the bowl of a food processor. Process until smooth. Keep the motor running and add the water in a steady stream until thoroughly blended. Serve at room temperature.

CHICKEN SATAY

MAKES 4 SKEWERS

Cut a skinless, boneless chicken breast into long, thin strips and thread on skewers that have been soaked in water for several hours. Season with salt and pepper. Brush the chicken with oil and broil until tender, about 4 minutes per side. Serve with the sauce.

Fruit and Nut Salsa with Roquefort

Here's an unusual salsa that is at its best stuffed into celery sticks or mounded on cucumber rounds. You'll also like it in a rollwich (see page 54), or with some cubed chicken for a light lunch.

MAKES 2 CUPS

1½ tablespoons olive oil
2 teaspoons dry mustard
1 cup walnut halves
½ cup chopped celery

1 large pear, peeled, cored, and diced
½ cup Roquefort cheese, crumbled
1 tablespoon honey
Salt and freshly ground pepper to taste

1. Heat the oil and dry mustard in a small pan over medium heat. Add the nuts and sauté until golden, 3 to 4 minutes. Transfer to a large bowl.

2. Add the remaining ingredients and stir. Season with the salt and pepper, and serve immediately.

Try substituting any of the following nut and cheese combinations:

- **Pecans and Gorgonzola**
- **Walnuts and goat cheese**
- **Hazelnuts and Gorgonzola**
- **Walnuts and Feta**

BASIL PESTO DIP

This versatile dip is excellent with crudités, as a stuffing for vegetables, as a spread for crostini, or even as a filling for finger sandwiches.

MAKES ¾ CUP

½ cup fresh basil leaves, washed and dried
1 tablespoon pignoli
1½ tablespoons freshly grated
* Parmesan cheese*

1 small clove garlic, minced
3 tablespoons extra-virgin olive oil
⅔ cup fat-free mayonnaise

1. Place the basil, nuts, cheese, and garlic in the bowl of a food processor. Process until finely chopped. While the motor is running, slowly pour in the olive oil until well blended. Transfer to a small bowl.

2. Stir the mayonnaise into the pesto, and mix well.

> **In a rush? Omit step 1 and all ingredients except mayonnaise. Stir ½ cup prepared pesto into the mayonnaise.**

BASIL PESTO WEDGES

MAKES 8 WEDGES

Spread a layer of Basil Pesto Dip on a prebaked pizza crust, like Boboli. Bake at 450°F for 10 to 15 minutes, until the crust is crisp and the topping is hot. Cut into wedges and serve.

BAKED CLAM DIP LOAF

Surround this impressive dip with crudités, breadsticks, and the leftover bread cubes.

MAKES 6 TO 8 SERVINGS

1 large (1½ pounds) unsliced round
 sourdough or black bread
4 containers (4 ounces each) herb or
 garlic cream cheese spread

1 cup mayonnaise
3 cans (6½ ounces) minced clams,
 drained
4 green onions, finely chopped

1. Preheat the oven to 350°F.

2. Cut a slice off the top of the bread, about 2 inches down. Reserve the lid. Remove the insides of the bread, leaving a 1-inch shell. Cut the insides into cubes, and set aside.

3. Using an electric mixer, beat the cream cheese spread and mayonnaise until blended. Stir in the clams and onions.

4. Spoon the mixture into the bread shell and cover with reserved lid. Wrap tightly in aluminum foil.

5. Bake about 1½ hours, until the filling is very hot and bread is crusty.

If you prefer, you can substitute canned lump crabmeat for the clams.

GARLIC AÏOLI

Aïoli is a flavored mayonnaise that makes a wonderful dip for fresh, slightly steamed or blanched vegetables. It also makes a great condiment for poached chicken or turkey sandwiches. Use homemade mayonnaise if you have any on hand.

MAKES ABOUT 1 CUP

7 cloves garlic, minced
1¼ tablespoons fresh lemon juice
1 tablespoon minced fresh herbs
  (optional)

1 tablespoon Dijon mustard
1 cup mayonnaise
Salt and freshly ground pepper to taste

1. Place the garlic, lemon juice, herbs, and mustard in a food processor, and blend well. Transfer to a bowl.

2. Add the mayonnaise and mix well. Season with salt and freshly ground pepper.

Stir in any of the following for variety:

- **Chopped sun-dried tomatoes**
- **Chopped roasted peppers**
- **A dash of hot sauce**

MARINATED ARTICHOKES AND MUSHROOMS

These are a good nibble. Surrounding them with crusty Italian bread, olives, tomato slices, and fresh mozzarella makes for an attractive antipasto platter.

MAKES ABOUT 2 CUPS

⅓ cup extra-virgin olive oil
1 tablespoon balsamic vinegar
2 tablespoons chopped fresh basil
1 large clove garlic, minced

2 jars (6 ounces) marinated artichokes
⅔ cup small white mushrooms, washed and brushed clean

1. Whisk together the oil, vinegar, basil, and garlic in a small bowl.

2. Add the artichokes and marinade and the mushrooms. Toss to combine. Cover and refrigerate for at least 4 hours.

MARINATED NIÇOISE OLIVES

Infused with a double dose of garlic, these olives are a wonderful nibble. Team with crusty Italian baguettes, good-quality olive oil, and Feta cheese.

MAKES ABOUT 2 CUPS

2 cups niçoise olives, drained
2 tablespoons olive oil
2 tablespoons garlic-flavored oil
2 tablespoons fresh chopped basil

2 sprigs fresh oregano
4 cloves garlic, peeled and slightly
   crushed
Freshly ground pepper to taste

Place all the ingredients in a bowl and mix until thoroughly combined. Place in a tightly sealed jar or plastic container and let marinate for at least 2 days, shaking occasionally.

BLACK OLIVADA

This simple olive spread has an intense flavor that goes a long way, so use sparingly. Add a tablespoon of capers if you have some on hand. My uncle, Stan Ryback, a real olive lover, gave me this simple advice: When buying olives, go for the highest quality. The difference in taste is tremendous and worth the price tag to someone who really savors these tasty tidbits.

MAKES ABOUT 1½ CUPS

2 cups kalamata or other imported olives in brine, drained and pitted

¼ cup extra-virgin olive oil
Freshly ground pepper to taste

Place the olives in the bowl of a food processor. Process until coarsely chopped. With the motor running, add the olive oil in a steady stream until you have a smooth paste. Add the pepper.

Serve Black Olivada with:

- **Goat cheese and sun-dried tomato slivers on crostini**
- **Fresh mozzarella on crostini**
- **Swiss cheese and chopped plum tomatoes on baguette slices**
- **Roasted pepper strips and fontina on crostini**
- **Radicchio on olive bread or toasted baguette**

ROQUEFORT BALL

This is one of my favorite cheese spreads. The sharp combination of blue cheese and walnuts is equally good on bread, piped onto pears, or stuffed into cherry tomatoes or mushroom caps.

MAKES ABOUT 6 SERVINGS

1 package (8 ounces) cream cheese, at
room temperature
4 ounces crumbled Roquefort cheese

2 tablespoons heavy cream
½ cup finely chopped walnuts
¼ cup plump raisins

1. Place the cream cheese, Roquefort, and cream in a food processor. Pulse, using on/off turns, until thoroughly combined, and transfer to a bowl. Stir in ¼ cup of the nuts. Shape into a ball, wrap, and refrigerate at least 3 hours, until firm.

2. Combine the remaining nuts and the raisins. Roll the cheese ball in the mixture, lightly pressing to adhere. Serve at room temperature.

A Roquefort Ball is a versatile spread. Here are some interesting uses:

- **Spread on tart apple slices.**
- **Spread on crostini, bagel chips, or bruschetta.**
- **Spoon into cherry tomatoes or mushroom caps. Broil until golden, about 5 minutes.**
- **Spread on cucumber slices.**
- **Spread a thin layer on thinly sliced smoked turkey. Top with a thin strip of roasted pepper. Roll and secure with a toothpick.**

BLUE CHEESE AND BACON TOASTS

MAKES 8

1 French baguette, halved lengthwise
Roquefort Ball (page 40), without
   raisin garnish

Freshly ground pepper to taste
4 slices of cooked bacon, crumbled

1. Preheat the broiler. Broil the bread halves, cut side up, until lightly toasted, 1 to 2 minutes.

2. Spread the cheese and walnut spread on the bread. Sprinkle with the pepper and bacon. Broil until the cheese bubbles. Cut each half into 4 pieces, and serve immediately.

GOAT CHEESE LOG WITH SUN-DRIED TOMATOES AND BASIL

This is a perfect spread on crostini. Feel free to substitute roasted peppers for the tomatoes.

MAKES ABOUT 6 SERVINGS

1 package (8 ounces) cream cheese, at room temperature

8 ounces goat cheese, at room temperature

¼ cup oil-packed sun-dried tomatoes, drained and thinly sliced

1 tablespoon finely chopped fresh basil

Extra-virgin olive oil

1. Combine the goat cheese and cream cheese in a food processor until blended. Stir in the sun-dried tomatoes. Refrigerate cheese mixture for 30 minutes.

2. Shape cheese mixture into a log about 2 inches in diameter. Use a knife to smooth the top and sides of the log. Make decorative lines with the sharp edge of the knife. Sprinkle on basil, and drizzle with olive oil. Serve at room temperature.

Wine and Cheese

This combination is simply perfect for a romantic evening at home, an intimate evening with friends, a formal party, before the theater, for anytime. And it's ready in minutes. Unless you are a wine connoisseur (or your guests are) simply mix and match. Most experts agree that you can't go wrong with red wine, and white wine makes a fine accompaniment to young cheeses. You may want to add some fresh fruit, crackers, crostini, baguettes, antipasto . . . your choices are almost endless. Oh, and don't forget some good music. Enjoy!

STUFFED BRIE

Serve on a platter surrounded by an assortment of crackers, flatbreads, and sliced fruit. When slicing Brie or soft cheese wheels, freeze the Brie for 1 hour, until firm, not frozen. Then slice with a long, sharp knife.

MAKES ABOUT 6 SERVINGS

1 package (8 ounces) cream cheese, at room temperature
1 tablespoon pesto
4 oil-packed sun-dried tomatoes, drained

3 tablespoons chopped marinated roasted peppers, drained
1 wheel (1 pound) Brie or Gouda

1. Cut the cream cheese in half and place each piece in a separate bowl.

2. Add the pesto to one bowl, and mix well. Refrigerate at least 30 minutes.

3. Place the remaining cream cheese, the tomatoes, and the peppers in a food processor and process until smooth. Transfer to a bowl and refrigerate for at least 30 minutes.

4. Carefully lay the wheel of cheese on its side and, using a long, sharp knife, horizontally cut into thirds.

5. Spread the pesto mixture on the bottom layer. Cover with the middle layer.

6. Spread the tomato mixture on the middle layer. Cover with the top layer. Gently press together. Cover with plastic wrap and refrigerate until set.

CAMEMBERT WITH APRICOT PRESERVES, PECANS, AND DRIED CRANBERRIES

This treat looks so festive, you'll want to serve it at all of your special occasions—and it's so easy! Serve chilled.

½ cup apricot preserves
1 wheel (½ pound) Camembert

¼ cup finely chopped pecans
⅓ cup dried cranberries

1. Spread the preserves on the sides of the Camembert wheel. Roll the cheese in the nuts, reserving 1 to 2 tablespoons for garnish.

2. Spread a layer of preserves on the top of the wheel. Cover with the dried cranberries and sprinkle on the remaining nuts. Serve on small baguette slices, crackers, celery sticks, or apple slices.

A Little Something

BAKED BRIE STUFFED WITH STRAWBERRY PRESERVES AND TOASTED ALMONDS

This impressive nibble is delicious, quick to make, and can be prepared in advance.

MAKES ABOUT 8 SERVINGS

1 wheel (2 to 3 pounds) of Brie
½ cup strawberry preserves
⅓ cup toasted almonds, finely chopped

1 pound frozen puff pastry, thawed
Vegetable oil cooking spray
1 egg yolk

1. Carefully lay the cheese on its side and using a long, sharp knife, horizontally cut in half.

2. Spread the preserves on the cut side of the bottom layer of cheese. Sprinkle on the nuts. Replace the top half of the brie.

3. Roll out the puff pastry into a circle, about double the diameter of the wheel of Brie. Place the Brie in the center of the pastry. Gather up the edges and decoratively twist together. Refrigerate for at least 1 hour or up to 24 hours wrapped in plastic.

4. Preheat the oven to 375°F. Spray a large baking sheet with cooking spray.

5. Beat the egg yolk and brush over the pastry. Bake about 40 minutes, until the pastry is evenly puffed and brown. Serve warm or at room temperature.

Marinated Goat Cheese with Crumb Crust

This treat pairs wonderfully with fresh fruit, olives, marinated mushrooms, roasted peppers, crostini, crackers, or baguette slices.

½ cup extra-virgin olive oil
2 tablespoons fresh oregano, chopped
Freshly ground pepper to taste
½ pound goat cheese, sliced into
*   1-inch-thick slices*

1 cup fresh bread crumbs
Salt to taste

1. Combine the olive oil and oregano in a small bowl. Season generously with pepper.

2. Pour the oil mixture onto the cheese slices, cover, and refrigerate for at least 3 hours.

3. Preheat the oven to 325°F.

4. Remove the cheese from the oil and dredge in the bread crumbs. Place on a foil-covered baking sheet and bake about 5 minutes, until the cheese begins to bubble around the edges.

SOUTHWESTERN MIX

This gives munching added zip—and has a lot less fat than buttered popcorn. The perfect snack to set out during your favorite ball game. Going, going, gone!

6 cups air-popped popcorn
1 cup salted peanuts
1 cup fat-free pretzel nuggets
2 tablespoons light margarine, melted
1 teaspoon chili powder

½ teaspoon garlic powder
¼ cup freshly grated Parmesan or
   cheddar cheese
Salt to taste

1. Preheat the oven to 300°F.

2. Place the popcorn, peanuts, and pretzels in a self-sealing plastic bag.

3. Combine the melted margarine, chili powder, and garlic powder in a small bowl. Pour on the popcorn mixture. Seal bag and shake to coat evenly.

4. Pour into a 9- by 13-inch baking pan, sprinkle on the cheese, and bake for 10 minutes. Cool completely. Season with salt. Store in an airtight container.

Caramel Munch

You can't get enough of this sweet and crunchy popcorn! Add a few cups of roasted peanuts if you like.

MAKES 8 CUPS

8 cups air-popped popcorn
¼ cup unsalted butter

¼ cup firmly packed brown sugar
¼ cup light molasses

1. Preheat the oven to 350°F. Place the popcorn in a 9- by 13-inch baking pan.

2. In a small saucepan, melt the butter over medium heat. Stir in the sugar and molasses. Bring to a boil, stirring constantly for about 1½ minutes. Pour evenly over the popcorn. Gently toss to coat evenly.

3. Bake about 15 minutes, stirring occasionally, until brown.

GRANOLA

This is a staple in my house. We eat it for breakfast, sprinkled over fresh fruit, mixed into a snack-size yogurt, or just by the handful! For a healthy after-school snack, spread a layer of peanut butter on apple slices and sprinkle on Granola.

MAKES ABOUT 3 CUPS

2 cups old-fashioned oats
1 cup coarsely chopped pecans or
   sliced almonds
⅔ cup raisins, dried cranberries, or
   dried cherries

5 tablespoons honey
1½ tablespoons vegetable oil
¾ teaspoon ground cinnamon

1. Preheat the oven to 325°F.

2. Combine the oats, nuts, and dried fruit in a large bowl.

3. Place the remaining ingredients in a small saucepan and bring to a boil, stirring constantly. Pour over the oatmeal mixture; stir to coat evenly.

4. Spread in a shallow baking pan. Bake at 325°F for 25 minutes, stirring frequently. Cool completely in the pan. Store in a large airtight container.

For variety, add some:

- **Chopped dried fruit**
- **Sunflower seeds**
- **Carob chips**

Orange Macadamia Nuts

These are a delicious nibble. Save the extras to toss into salads. If you prefer, walnuts or pecans can be substituted for macadamia nuts.

MAKES 2 CUPS

2 tablespoons unsalted butter
1½ tablespoons grated orange zest
1 teaspoon ground cinnamon

2 cups unsalted macadamia nuts
2 tablespoons sugar
1 teaspoon salt

1. Preheat the oven to 300°F. Line a baking sheet with aluminum foil.

2. Melt the butter in a saucepan over medium heat. Add the orange zest and cinnamon, and stir until dissolved and aromatic.

3. Stir in the remaining ingredients, and transfer to a baking sheet.

4. Bake, stirring occasionally, about 20 minutes, until the nuts are toasted.

GLAZED WALNUTS

These are equally good nibbling while watching your favorite video or at a formal cocktail party. The recipe also works well with peanuts or pecans.

MAKES 2 CUPS

Vegetable oil cooking spray
2 cups walnut halves
¼ cup sugar

1 tablespoon soy sauce
2 tablespoons unsalted butter, melted

1. Preheat the oven to 250°F. Spray a baking sheet with cooking spray.

2. Soak the walnuts in a large bowl of hot water for 5 minutes, and drain well.

3. Combine the remaining ingredients in a bowl. Add the nuts and stir to coat evenly.

4. Spread nuts on baking sheet. Bake for 30 to 40 minutes, stirring occasionally, until shiny and golden. Let cool.

Something More

There are times when munching, crunching, and nibbling just don't hit the spot. It may not be mealtime—it might even be midnight—but you're hungry for more than a little something.

These recipes are comforting and substantial. They're just the thing for a casual party, a night of television, or a midnight refrigerator raid. So, forget fast food—these recipes are quick to make and a whole lot tastier.

TURKEY CRANBERRY ROLLWICH

I ate my first "rollwich"—a large flour tortilla loaded with fabulous fillings—while vacationing on Cape Cod with friends and family. It makes a perfect late-night munch or, cut into quarters, a casual hors d'oeuvre. Half a sandwich is the perfect munch for casual cocktails, appetizers during the big game, a coffee break during household chores—it is perfect for just about any occasion.

MAKES 3 SANDWICHES

3 large flour tortillas
2 tablespoons regular or fat-free
  mayonnaise
⅓ cup canned whole cranberry sauce
  or cranberry chutney

9 thin slices of deli turkey breast
½ cup shredded lettuce
9 thin plum tomato slices

1. Lay the tortillas on a flat surface. Combine the mayonnaise and cranberry sauce or chutney in a small bowl.

2. Divide the cranberry mixture among the tortillas and spread evenly.

3. Top with the turkey, lettuce, and tomato.

4. Starting at one end, roll up each tortilla. Fold up a flap on one end of each tortilla so it can easily be held.

Here are some other nice fillings:

- **Roast beef, provolone cheese, lettuce, tomato slices, mayonnaise**
- **Turkey, white horseradish, mayonnaise, onion slices, tomato slices**
- **Tomato slices, onion slices, shredded carrots, lettuce, avocado slices, mayonnaise**
- **Turkey, cooked bacon strips, Monterey Jack cheese, lettuce, tomato slices, mayonnaise**
- **Fruit and Nut Salsa with Roquefort (page 33), and canned tuna mixed with mayonnaise**

OPEN-FACED ROAST BEEF SANDWICH

This updated "hero" will get rid of the hunger pangs without weighing you down. It's great during a late-night poker game.

MAKES 2 SANDWICHES

1 tablespoon mayonnaise
2 teaspoons white horseradish
2 large pieces flat Middle Eastern bread

¼ cup chopped red onion
4 ounces sliced roast beef

1. Mix the mayonnaise and horseradish together in a small bowl. Spread a thin layer on each piece of bread.

2. Divide the onions and sprinkle over the horseradish mixture. Top with the roast beef. Fold in half and eat as a sandwich, or cut with a fork and knife.

Tex-Mex Hot Dogs

These are a great munch during the big game.

MAKES 4

4 grilled or boiled frankfurters
4 flour tortillas
½ cup Tomato Salsa (page 28),
    or your favorite salsa

½ cup shredded cheddar cheese
Vegetable oil cooking spray

1. Preheat the broiler.

2. Place a frank on top of each tortilla.

3. Top with the salsa and cheese, and roll up. Place on a baking sheet and spray with the cooking spray. Broil until the cheese melts, about 1 minute.

GRILLED FONTINA, SUN-DRIED TOMATO, AND BACON SANDWICH

A glass of chocolate milk goes nicely with this gourmet take on an old favorite.

1 tablespoon sun-dried tomatoes
  packed in oil, drained and chopped,
  or 2 tablespoons plum tomatoes,
  seeded and chopped
1 small clove garlic, minced

Two ½-inch-thick baguette slices
2 slices Brie or fontina cheese
2 thin slices cooked bacon
Olive oil or olive oil cooking spray

1. In a small bowl, combine the tomatoes and the garlic.

2. Top 1 baguette slice with 1 slice of cheese, the tomatoes, and the bacon. Cover with the remaining slice of cheese and bread. Brush both sides of sandwich with the olive oil or cooking spray.

3. Heat a nonstick skillet over medium heat and cook until golden brown and cheese melts, pressing occasionally with a spatula, about 4 minutes per side.

CALIFORNIA GRILLED SANDWICH

Two ½-inch-thick baguette slices
1 tablespoon Green Sauce (page 29)
2 tablespoons alfalfa sprouts
2 tablespoons plum tomatoes, seeded
   and chopped

2 slices white cheddar cheese
Olive oil or olive oil cooking spray

1. Top the baguette slices with the green sauce, sprouts, tomatoes, and cheese. Brush with the oil.

2. Heat a nonstick skillet over medium heat and cook until golden brown and the cheese melts, pressing occasionally with a spatula, about 4 minutes per side.

> A quick way to cook bacon is to place 2 slices on a paper-lined plate, cover with a paper towel, and microwave at high for about 2 minutes. Increase the amount of time if you add more bacon.

TOMATO SANDWICH

This was a favorite in my house while growing up. We used iceberg lettuce, but now I prefer it with bitter greens, like arugula.

4 slices white bread, toasted
¼ cup reduced-fat mayonnaise or
  Bacon Mayonnaise

½ cup arugula, tough stems removed
1 vine-ripened red tomato, sliced
Salt and freshly ground pepper to taste

1. On each slice of bread, spread a layer of mayonnaise.

2. For each sandwich, layer arugula and tomato slices on 2 slices of bread. Season with salt and pepper. Cover with the remaining bread. Cut in half crosswise.

Variations

- **Add thin slices of red onion and substitute Spicy Dipping Sauce (page 76) for the mayonnaise.**

- **Omit the mayonnaise and substitute 2 to 4 tablespoons of Green Sauce (page 29).**

BACON MAYONNAISE

MAKES ½ CUP

3 slices crisp cooked bacon, chopped
½ cup mayonnaise

1 tablespoon Dijon mustard

Mix the ingredients together in a small bowl until thoroughly combined.

PRETZEL ROLLS

Easy to make, quick to eat, and healthy—this is the perfect after-school snack or late-night munch.

MAKES 2

2 slices of your favorite cheese

2 slices of your favorite fat-free cold cuts

Mustard

2 salted pretzel rods

1. Place the cold cut slices on a flat work surface. Top with the cheese slices. Spread a thin layer of mustard on top of cheese.

2. Place pretzel rods at bottom edge of cheese and roll cheese and cold cuts around the pretzels.

Variation
Omit mustard and spread a layer of light cream cheese on one side of the cheese before rolling.

CHOPPED EGGS, MUSHROOMS, AND ONIONS ON BLACK BREAD

My mother, Esty Moskowitz, loved her delicious egg salad on crackers for hors d'oeuvres or on black bread for a snack or light lunch.

MAKES 8 SERVINGS

2 tablespoons olive oil
1 small onion, chopped
½ cup chopped mushrooms

4 hard-boiled eggs
Salt and freshly ground pepper to taste
4 slices black bread

1. Heat the oil in a medium skillet over medium-high heat. Sauté the onions and mushrooms about 6 minutes, until the onions are translucent and mushrooms are tender.

2. Chop the eggs and add the mushroom mixture and juices. Season with salt and pepper. If the mixture is too dry, add a few drops of olive oil.

3. Spread mixture on each slice of bread, and cut into triangles.

VEGETABLE FRITTATA ON BAGUETTE

Here's a gourmet version of "eggs on a roll"—you'll love the improvements. Feel free to substitute your favorite filling for the vegetables. I like sautéed spinach and mushrooms, chopped fresh herbs, caponata, or grilled vegetables.

MAKES 4 SERVINGS

2 tablespoons butter

1 small onion, chopped

¼ cup chopped mushrooms

¼ cup frozen peas, thawed

3 eggs

1 tablespoon freshly grated Parmesan
    cheese

Salt and freshly ground pepper to taste

1 tablespoon olive oil

2 large baguettes, split in half

1 tablespoon Basil Pesto Dip (page 34)
    or butter

1. In a small skillet, melt the butter over medium heat. Add the onions and mushrooms. Cook, stirring constantly, about 4 minutes, until the onions are translucent. Add the peas and set aside.

2. Combine the eggs, Parmesan, salt, and pepper in a bowl. Beat well.

3. Add the vegetable mixture and mix well.

4. Place the olive oil in a nonstick frying pan over high heat. Pour in the egg mixture and cook, lifting the edges with a spatula and tipping the pan to allow the uncooked eggs to flow under and cook. Lower the heat, cover, and continue to cook 2 to 4 minutes, until the eggs are set. Invert the frittata onto a plate and allow to cool.

5. Cut the frittata in half and place on the bottom halves of the baguettes. Spread Basil Pesto Dip over the tops of the baguettes, cover the frittata with the top halves, and cut in half crosswise.

Romaine Burritos with Blue Cheese, Chicken, Apples, and Pecans

Romaine, radicchio, butter, or iceberg lettuce leaves are great low-calorie "wrappers." Make a platter for your next get-together or whip one up for a snack or light lunch.

MAKES 8

4 ounces cooked chicken, diced
2 ounces blue cheese, crumbled
1 apple, peeled, cored, and diced
¼ cup chopped pecans

2 tablespoons prepared Dijon mustard
salad dressing or vinaigrette
8 romaine lettuce leaves, hard stem
removed

1. Combine the chicken, blue cheese, apple, and pecans in a small bowl, and toss with the dressing.

2. Place the romaine on a flat work surface. Place a tablespoon of filling about ¼ inch from the wide end of each leaf. Roll up burrito style, completely enclosing the filling.

Some other nice stuffings:

- **Tomato Salsa (page 28) mixed with diced chicken**
- **Goat Cheese Log with Sun-dried Tomatoes and Basil (page 42)**
- **Dilled Shrimp Salad (page 94)**
- **Chopped Eggs, Mushrooms, and Onions (page 61)**

BROCCOLI AND CHEESE BREAD

This is great as a casual snack or an elegant hors d'oeuvre. Cut the loaf into larger pieces when you need something more, or team it with a bowl of soup. Cut it into smaller pieces for hors d'oeuvres. Add some chopped sun-dried tomatoes or roasted peppers if you like.

MAKES 2 LOAVES

Vegetable oil cooking spray
1 package (10 ounces) chopped frozen
   broccoli, thawed and squeezed of
   excess water
½ cup thinly sliced green onions
1 large egg, beaten
2 tablespoons milk

1 tablespoon chopped fresh dill
¼ teaspoon ground nutmeg
2 cups grated cheddar cheese
¼ cup fresh bread crumbs
1 to 2 tablespoons flour
1 tube (11 ounces) crusty French bread
   dough, refrigerated

1. Preheat the oven to 375°F. Spray a baking sheet with the cooking spray.

2. Mix the broccoli, green onions, egg, milk, dill, and nutmeg in a bowl until combined. Add the cheese and bread crumbs.

3. Sprinkle flour over a pastry board and unroll the dough. Roll out into a 13-inch square. Cut in half to form two equal rectangles, 6 by 13 inches. Divide the filling and place down the center of each rectangle. For each rectangle, fold one side over filling. Fold over remaining side, pressing the seam to seal. Seal the two ends of the loaves. Cut slits down the tops of the loaves to let air escape.

4. Bake about 25 minutes, until golden brown. Let cool slightly and cut into pieces.

GOURMET ENGLISH MUFFINS

These are great midday when the kids are hungry after school, or when you need a midnight snack. Quick and delicious, they won't weigh you down.

MAKES 2

2 English muffins, split in half and lightly toasted
Any of the following toppings

Goat Cheese and Sun-dried Tomato Muffins
3 to 4 tablespoons Goat Cheese Log with Sun-dried Tomatoes and Basil (page 42)

or

2 ounces soft goat cheese
2 tablespoons sun-dried tomatoes, packed in oil, drained, and chopped
1 tablespoon chopped basil or ½ teaspoon dried basil

Cream Cheese, Tomato, and Red Onion Muffins
2 tablespoons cream cheese
2 thin slices tomato
2 thin slices red onion

Pizza Muffins
2 tablespoons prepared pizza or spaghetti sauce
¼ cup shredded mozzarella cheese
Salt, pepper, and garlic powder to taste

Tuna Melt Muffins
1 cup tuna fish salad
¼ cup shredded cheddar cheese

1. Spread or layer the toppings on the muffins in the order listed.

2. Broil 1 to 2 minutes, until edges are golden brown and the toppings are warm.

FINGER SANDWICHES

Treat yourself or impress a crowd with these tiny sandwiches. Serve with lemonade, flavored iced teas, flavored coffees, and espresso specialties. A nice platter of sweets (see Something Sweet, page 119) would also be nice.

MAKES 8 SANDWICHES

Cream Cheese and Cucumber Sandwiches
8 thin slices of good-quality white, pumpernickel, wheat, or multi-grain bread, crusts neatly cut away
¼ cup light cream cheese
Freshly ground pepper to taste
1 cucumber, peeled and thinly sliced
Zest of 1 orange, julienned

Honey Mustard and Turkey Sandwiches
8 thin slices of good-quality white, pumpernickel, wheat, or multi-grain bread, crusts neatly cut away

1½ tablespoons prepared honey mustard or raspberry mustard
8 thin slices cooked turkey or deli turkey

Pesto Cream and Sun-dried Tomato Sandwiches
8 thin slices of good-quality white, pumpernickel, wheat, or multi-grain bread, crusts neatly cut away
¼ cup Basil Pesto Dip (page 34)
16 sun-dried tomatoes, soaked in water for 15 minutes, drained and sliced

Carefully spread and layer ingredients on half the bread in the order listed. Cover with the remaining bread. Cut each sandwich diagonally in half. Arrange decoratively on a platter.

Here are some other combinations:

- Chutney and deli roast beef or turkey
- Roquefort Ball (page 40) and deli turkey
- Cream cheese mixed with finely chopped vegetables

- Smoked Salmon Spread (page 109)
- A thin layer of mayonnaise, sliced radishes, and dill
- Poached chicken and Dijon mustard

PERSONAL PIZZAS

Just about everyone loves pizza. These gooey triangles and squares are even popping up at elegant restaurants; we can't seem to get enough and are willing to experiment with just about any topping or crust. The wide availability of purchased baked cheese pizza crusts makes preparing homemade pizza simple. Here are some of my favorite creations. Or create your own . . . anything goes!

4 individual-size Boboli or baked cheese pizza crusts
Olive oil
Any of the following toppings

Pesto, Olive, and Artichoke Pizza
½ cup Sun-dried Tomato and Roasted Pepper Pesto (page 85) or prepared basil pesto
1½ cups shredded mozzarella cheese
1 cup pitted Greek olives, halved
1 jar (3½ ounces) artichoke hearts packed in oil, drained and quartered

Smoked Salmon Pizza*
4 ounces mild goat cheese
2 tablespoons sour cream
1 tablespoon chopped fresh dill
1 small red onion, thinly sliced
6 ounces thinly sliced smoked salmon

Tomato and Cheese Pizza
1½ cups shredded mozzarella cheese
6 ripe plum tomatoes, peeled, seeded, and chopped
4 prepared anchovy fillets packed in oil, drained, and cut in half (optional)
Salt, pepper, and chopped fresh basil to taste

*Bake the pizza shell for 10 minutes, layer on the toppings, and serve. The toppings are not baked.

1. Preheat the oven to 450°F. Brush the pizza shells with olive oil.

2. Layer on ingredients in the order listed. Drizzle with additional olive oil if desired.

3. Bake at 450°F about 10 minutes, until the cheese is melted and the ingredients are heated throughout.

PIZZA PARTY

Instead of making the pizzas in advance, let guests create their own. Set out a variety of toppings, sauces, and ready-made pizza crusts. Offer some of your favorite combinations and let the fun begin.

Unusual Pizzas

For the times you want something with extra pizzazz, experiment with one of these interesting combinations. They are a great conversation piece at parties.

1 large purchased baked pita crust
1 large loaf French bread, cut in half
4 pita bread rounds or English muffins,
  split in half
Any of the following toppings

Barbecue Chicken Pizza
½ cup prepared barbecue sauce
1 cup shredded cooked chicken
1 cup shredded smoked mozzarella
  cheese

Tex-Mex Pizza
⅔ cup Tomato Salsa (page 28) or your
  favorite salsa
¾ cup shredded cooked chicken or beef
1 cup shredded cheddar cheese
1 to 2 tablespoons chopped pickled
  jalapeño peppers

Salad Pizza
½ cup shredded fontina cheese
½ cup shredded mozzarella cheese
2 cups shredded lettuce
1 small tomato, seeded and chopped
2 tablespoons fat-free Italian dressing
2 tablespoons freshly grated Parmesan
  cheese

Chicken, Apple, and Cheddar Pizza
2 apples, cored, peeled, and thinly sliced
1 cup shredded cooked chicken or turkey
1 cup shredded cheddar cheese

Greek Pizza
1 cup shredded mozzarella cheese
2 plum tomatoes, thinly sliced
1 cup crumbled Feta cheese
½ cup brine-cured pitted kalamata olives,
  halved
1 teaspoon oregano

Preheat the oven to 400°F. Layer or spread the ingredients on the baked pizza crust, French bread, pita bread rounds, or English muffins. Bake until the toppings are hot, about 10 minutes.

PITA PIZZA

These pizzas take less time to make than a trip to the local pizzeria and are just as delicious and a lot healthier. They make fabulous hors d'oeuvres and a great after-school snack.

MAKES 8 SERVINGS

4 pita breads
Any of the following toppings

Tomato Garlic Pizza
½ cup tomato or pizza sauce
¾ cup low-fat shredded mozzarella
  cheese
1 ripe plum tomato, thinly sliced
1 garlic clove, minced

Mexican Pizza
1 cup Black Bean Dip (page 27) or
  fat-free bean dip
½ cup Mexican salsa
¾ cup shredded reduced-fat Monterey
  Jack cheese

White Pizza
1 cup low-fat creamy ricotta cheese
¾ cup low-fat shredded mozzarella
  cheese
2 cloves garlic, minced

1. Preheat the oven to 375°F.

2. Using small kitchen scissors or a knife, carefully split each pita round along the edge into 2 equal circles. Place on a baking sheet and bake for 5 minutes.

3. Layer the remaining ingredients on the pita rounds in the order listed. Bake at 375°F for 10 minutes, or until the cheese melts.

STUFFED POTATO SKINS

Scooped-out baked potatoes make terrific shells for your favorite stuffing. Two of these and a mug of beer makes a great snack during the big game.

MAKES 4

4 large Idaho potatoes, washed and
    scrubbed
Olive oil

1 cup shredded cheddar cheese
8 strips cooked bacon, chopped

1. Preheat the oven to 450°F. Use a fork to pierce the potatoes. Bake the potatoes for about 1 hour.

2. Split each potato in half. Using a spoon or melon baller, scoop out the insides leaving a thin layer of potato attached to the skin. Brush the skins inside and out with a layer of olive oil.

3. Sprinkle on the cheese and bacon.

4. Bake at 450°F for about 10 minutes, until the cheese melts. Garnish with sour cream if desired.

Try these variations. For the cheddar cheese and bacon, you can substitute the following:

- **For Fontina and Sun-dried Tomato Skins:** 1 cup shredded fontina cheese and ¼ cup sun-dried tomatoes packed in oil, drained and chopped
- **For Pizza Skins:** 1 cup shredded mozzarella cheese, ½ cup chopped tomatoes, 1 tablespoon minced garlic, and salt, pepper, and oregano to taste

- **For Mexican Skins:** ½ cup prepared Mexican salsa, 1 cup shredded Monterey Jack cheese, and 2 tablespoons pickled jalapeño peppers, chopped

Bake as directed above.

BUFFALO CHICKEN WINGS

These red-hot wings got their start in Buffalo, but the taste has caught on like wild-fire. You'll need a good blue cheese dressing for dipping and plenty of drinks to put out the fire.

MAKES 6 SERVINGS

3 pounds chicken wings, tips removed, washed and patted dry
Salt and freshly ground pepper to taste
½ to 1 cup Frank's Original Red Hot sauce or your favorite hot pepper sauce
⅓ cup melted butter

Vegetable oil for frying
2 cups celery sticks, trimmed and cut into thin strips
1 package (1 pound) baby carrots
1 bottle (8 ounces) of your favorite blue cheese dressing

1. Season the chicken with salt and pepper. Combine the hot sauce and the butter in a large metal bowl and set aside.

2. Pour about 2 inches of oil into a large, heavy saucepan. Heat to 375°F. Cook the chicken thoroughly in batches until golden and crisp, about 10 minutes.

3. Quickly place the hot chicken wings into the hot sauce mixture and toss to coat. Serve with the celery, carrots, and blue cheese dressing.

CRISPY ONION RINGS WITH
SPICY DIPPING SAUCE

These restaurant-style onion rings are similar to the onion loaves that are popular at steak and rib houses. Make a large batch—they will disappear quickly!

MAKES 4 TO 6 SERVINGS

2 large onions, thinly sliced
1 cup buttermilk
2 cups flour
1 tablespoon salt

1 teaspoon freshly ground pepper
2 teaspoons paprika
Vegetable oil for frying
Spicy Dipping Sauce (page 76)

1. Separate the onions into circles and place in a large bowl. Add the buttermilk and toss to coat. Cover and refrigerate for at least 1 hour. Pour into a colander and drain.

2. Mix the flour, salt, pepper, and paprika in a large bowl. Add the onions and toss to cover with flour. Shake off the excess flour.

3. In a large nonstick skillet, pour the vegetable oil to a depth of 3 inches and heat to 350°F. Carefully place half the onions in the pan.

4. Fry for 3 minutes. Using a large spatula, turn over the onions in large chunks. Fry an additional 3 minutes, until brown and crispy. Carefully transfer onto paper towels and drain. Repeat with remaining onions. Serve with dipping sauce.

Use a mandoline to slice the onions. It is easier, and the onions will have a uniform thickness.

SPICY DIPPING SAUCE

This sauce is also a nice accompaniment to Oven-fried Zucchini (page 77).

This sauce is also a nice accompaniment to Oven-fried Zucchini (page 77).

MAKES 1 CUP

¼ *cup ketchup*
½ *cup mayonnaise*

2 to 3 tablespoons white horseradish
½ teaspoon cayenne pepper (optional)

Mix all the ingredients together in a small bowl until thoroughly combined.

QUICK CURRY DIPPING SAUCE

For the ketchup and cayenne pepper, if using, substitute ½ cup plain yogurt and 2 tea-spoons curry paste or curry powder. Mix until thoroughly combined.

OVEN-FRIED ZUCCHINI

The secret to the zucchini's crispiness is double dipping in egg whites—finally, double dipping is acceptable! These are excellent with Horseradish Yogurt Sauce or prepared tomato sauce.

MAKES 4 SERVINGS

Vegetable oil cooking spray
¼ cup seasoned dry bread crumbs
2 tablespoons freshly grated Parmesan
  cheese

1 cup zucchini, cut into ¼-inch wedges
2 large egg whites

1. Preheat the oven to 450°F. Liberally spray a baking sheet with vegetable cooking spray.

2. Combine the bread crumbs and Parmesan in a large bowl. Set aside.

3. Dip the zucchini in the egg whites and then coat with the bread-crumb mixture. Repeat.

4. Place on the prepared baking sheet, and spray liberally with cooking spray. Bake until golden, about 30 minutes. Serve with Horseradish Yogurt Sauce.

HORSERADISH YOGURT SAUCE

MAKES 1 CUP

1 cup plain nonfat yogurt

1 to 2 tablespoons white horseradish,
  to taste

Combine the yogurt and horseradish in a small bowl. Serve with the zucchini.

Quesadillas

These make terrific hors d'oeuvres or can be served with some Mexican rice or refried beans for dinner. Top with a dollop of sour cream, guacamole, or salsa. Island Delights (page 164) or Frozen Fruit Shakes (page 165) make a nice accompaniment.

MAKES 4 SERVINGS

4 flour tortillas
Vegetable oil cooking spray
Any of the following toppings

Cheese Quesadillas
1 cup shredded cheddar cheese

Cheese and Bean Quesadillas
1 cup canned refried beans
1 cup shredded Monterey Jack cheese

Brie and Mango Quesadillas
6 ounces Brie, sliced
1 ripe mango, pitted, peeled, and chopped
½ cup diced red onion
⅓ cup chopped red bell pepper
6 slices pickled jalapeño peppers
Salt and pepper to taste

Spicy Cheese Quesadillas
1 cup shredded Monterey Jack cheese
2 ounces chopped canned green chiles
1 small red onion, thinly sliced
1 prepared roasted pepper, cut into strips
Salt and pepper to taste

Sun-dried Tomato Quesadillas
2 tablespoons Sun-dried Tomato and Roasted Pepper Pesto (page 85)
1 cup shredded mozzarella cheese

BLT Quesadillas
4 tablespoons mayonnaise
4 slices cooked bacon, chopped
4 leaves romaine lettuce, shredded
½ cup seeded and chopped tomatoes
Pinch of salt and pepper

1. Divide the ingredients and layer in the order listed on half of each tortilla. Season with salt and pepper. Fold over the empty half of the tortilla to enclose filling. Place on a baking sheet.

2. Coat the tortillas with cooking spray. Broil about 5 inches from the heat for 1 minute. Turn over, coat with spray, and broil for an additional minute.

NACHOS

Nachos are a favorite munch anytime—while playing a game, watching a movie, or entertaining a large crowd. Remember to make a lot—these go quickly.

24 large tortilla chips
Sour cream for garnish (optional)
Prepared guacamole or Green Sauce
　(page 29) (optional)
Tomato Salsa (page 28) or your
　favorite salsa (optional)
Any of the following toppings

Cheese Nachos
8 ounces shredded cheddar cheese or
　Monterey Jack cheese
24 slices pickled jalapeño peppers

Nachos Grandes
1 can (15 ounces) refried beans or
　2 cups leftover chili
8 ounces shredded cheddar cheese or
　Monterey Jack cheese
24 slices pickled jalapeño peppers

California Nachos
9 ounces crumbled mild goat cheese,
　at room temperature
2 tablespoons finely chopped fresh
　cilantro
12 sun-dried tomatoes, packed in oil,
　drained and thinly sliced

Italian-style Nachos
8 ounces shredded mozzarella cheese
½ cup tomato sauce
¼ cup chopped fresh basil

1. Preheat the oven to 400°F. Arrange the tortilla chips on a baking sheet in a single layer.

2. Divide the remaining ingredients and layer on each chip.

3. Bake for 5 to 7 minutes, until the cheese melts. Garnish with sour cream, guacamole, or salsa, if desired.

Something for Entertaining

It's party time. Whether yours is a gathering of six or sixty, finger foods and light appetizers are the perfect "little something" to eat while chatting with a few friends, celebrating a birthday, or trying to impress a prospective client.

The following recipes are elegant yet easy to prepare; many can be made well in advance of the your first arrivals. You'll have plenty of time to enjoy the festivities.

CROSTINI TOPPED WITH SUN-DRIED TOMATO AND ROASTED PEPPER PESTO AND GOAT CHEESE

Crostini are similar to bruschetta, but smaller and thinner. Use your imagination and create your own favorite combinations.

MAKES ABOUT 24

1 large Italian or French bread
  baguette, cut into ¼-inch slices
1 tablespoon olive oil

1 cup Sun-dried Tomato and Roasted
  Pepper Pesto (page 85)
½ cup crumbled goat cheese (optional)

1. Preheat the oven to 400°F.

2. Brush bread tops with olive oil, and place on a baking sheet.

3. Bake about 8 minutes, until crisp but not hard throughout. Spread on the pesto in a thin layer and sprinkle on the goat cheese. Return to the oven and broil for 1 minute, until the cheese melts.

Some other nice toppings:

- **Honey, Brie, and apple slices**
- **Basil pesto, chopped tomatoes, arugula, and freshly grated Parmesan cheese**
- **Caponata**
- **Goat cheese and chopped fresh rosemary**

- **Smoked Salmon Spread and chopped fresh dill**
- **Garlic oil, salami, and provolone cheese**
- **Chopped tomatoes and shredded fresh mozzarella**

Sun-dried Tomato and Roasted Pepper Pesto

This wonderful pesto is delicious spread on Crostini (page 84) and Bagel Chips (page 23) or layered on pizza. For an interesting topping, mix the pesto with chopped kalamata olives.

MAKES 1 CUP

½ cup sun-dried tomatoes, packed in oil, drained
½ cup roasted peppers, drained

1 clove garlic, minced
2 tablespoons olive oil
1 tablespoon balsamic vinegar

Place the tomatoes, peppers, and garlic in the bowl of a food processor. Process 10 to 15 seconds, until the mixture reaches desired consistency. Add the remaining ingredients, and pulse to combine.

TOMATO BRUSCHETTA

Crusty and delicious, these make wonderful hors d'oeuvres and are excellent with an antipasto.

1 large loaf Italian bread or country bread, cut diagonally into ¾-inch slices

1 clove garlic, cut in half

1 to 2 tablespoons extra virgin olive oil or flavored oil

¾ cup vine-ripened chopped tomatoes

¼ cup chopped fresh basil

Salt and freshly ground pepper to taste

1. Preheat the broiler or toaster oven. Broil the bread for 1 to 2 minutes per side, until toasted.

2. Rub the cut garlic clove on top of the toasted bread. Drizzle oil on the bread. Top with the remaining ingredients.

Some other nice toppings:

- **Soft goat cheese, arugula, and toasted pine nuts**
- **Julienne roasted peppers and ⅓ cup chopped Greek olives**
- **Garlic oil and thin slices of prosciutto**
- **Roquefort Ball (page 40)**

HAM AND SWISS COCKTAIL SANDWICHES

Vacuum-packed cocktail bread stays fresh for at least two weeks, making it the perfect food to have on hand for drop-in guests. I always keep a few loaves in the freezer just in case . . .

MAKES 20 SANDWICHES

1 loaf (16 ounces) cocktail rye,
pumpernickel, or honey wheat bread
2 tablespoons butter, melted
¼ cup deli-style mustard

½ pound thinly sliced smoked ham,
cut in half
½ cup cornichons, cut in half
lengthwise
½ pound Swiss cheese, cut into squares

1. Preheat the oven to 400°F. Place the slices of cocktail bread on a large baking sheet. Brush both sides of each slice lightly with melted butter.

2. Spread one side of half the bread slices with mustard. Top with a piece of ham, a cornichon half, and a square of cheese, and then top with the remaining bread.

3. Bake about 10 minutes, until the cheese is melted. Cut into triangles, if desired.

Some other fabulous fillings:

- **Black Olivada (page 39) topped with Monterey Jack cheese, goat cheese, or smoked mozzarella squares**
- **Goat Cheese Log with Sun-dried Tomatoes and Basil (page 42) and cooked turkey breast**

- **Brie topped with your favorite preserves**
- **Sun-dried Tomato and Roasted Pepper Pesto (page 85) with smoked Gouda**

FOCACCIA IN A SNAP

Just snap open some frozen pizza dough, sprinkle on some easy-to-make toppings, and bake "homemade" focaccia in less than 30 minutes.

MAKES 6 TO 8 PIECES

1 roll (15 ounces) refrigerated pizza dough
Any of the following toppings
Salt and freshly ground pepper to taste

Roasted Pepper Focaccia
2 fresh or jarred roasted peppers, thinly sliced
1 to 2 tablespoons extra-virgin olive oil

Onion Focaccia
3 large onions, thinly sliced and sautéed in olive oil until brown
1 to 2 tablespoons extra-virgin olive oil

Puttanesca Focaccia
1 cup chopped kalamata olives
3 plum tomatoes, seeded and chopped
1 to 2 tablespoons extra-virgin olive oil to taste

1. Preheat the oven to 425°F. Remove the dough from the package and roll out on a 15- by 10-inch jelly roll pan. Press evenly into pan.

2. Sprinkle toppings evenly over the dough and drizzle with olive oil. Season with salt and freshly ground pepper. Bake about 20 minutes, until the crust is crisp and golden brown. Cut into rectangles and serve.

BREADSTICKS WITH PROSCIUTTO AND ROBIOLA

The savory, fresh taste of Robiola, a creamy mild cheese from Italy, goes nicely with the smokiness of prosciutto.

MAKES 30

8 ounces Robiola
30 crunchy breadsticks,
    about 5 inches each

1 pound thinly sliced prosciutto

1. Spread a thin layer of Robiola on each breadstick.

2. Cut each slice of prosciutto into 3 strips. Wrap a strip around each breadstick. Place decoratively on a platter and serve.

The wonderful texture and taste of prosciutto makes it the perfect choice for wrapping a variety of foods. Try it around:

- **Melon wedges**
- **Blanched chilled asparagus**
- **Steamed zucchini wedges**
- **Cheese and roasted pepper strips**

For a lovely platter, arrange the breadsticks with Robiola and prosciutto, alternating with Garlic and Cheese Twists (page 25).

CHERRY TOMATOES WITH VEGETABLE CRABMEAT FILLING

These "pop'ems" are excellent when cherry tomatoes are at their peak.

MAKES 30

2 cans (6 ounces each) lump crabmeat, picked over and drained of all excess liquid
½ cup light mayonnaise
2 green onions, finely chopped
½ yellow bell pepper, finely chopped

¼ cup shredded carrot
2 teaspoons chopped fresh parsley
2 teaspoons fresh lemon juice
Salt and freshly ground pepper to taste
30 cherry tomatoes

1. Finely chop the crabmeat in a large bowl.

2. Mix the crabmeat, mayonnaise, onions, bell pepper, carrot, parsley, lemon juice, salt, and pepper in a small bowl. Set aside.

3. Using a small sharp knife, cut a thin slice from the bottom of each tomato so they will stand. Cut a thin slice off the top, and scoop out the seeds and pulp with a small spoon.

4. Spoon about 1 teaspoon of filling into each tomato, arrange on a platter, and serve.

Other nice stuffings for cherry tomatoes are

- **Goat Cheese Log with Sun-dried Tomatoes and Basil (page 42)**
- **Chopped Eggs, Mushrooms, and Onions (page 61)**
- **Smoked Salmon Spread (page 109)**
- **Horseradish Tuna (page 92)**

For extra-special occasions, fill the cherry tomatoes with sour cream mixed with chopped chives. Top with caviar.

ZUCCHINI ROLLS

These appetizers are attractive, easy to prepare, and light—perfect for your health-conscious guests. Feel free to substitute eggplant.

MAKES 20

2 small zucchini, cut lengthwise into
   ¼-inch slices
⅔ cup fat-free Italian dressing
Vegetable oil cooking spray
1 jar (7½ ounces) roasted peppers, cut
   into thin strips

1 bunch arugula, stems removed
¼ cup freshly grated Parmesan cheese
   (optional)

1. Combine the zucchini and dressing in a large bowl. Cover and marinate for at least 1 hour.

2. Preheat the broiler or grill. Coat a large baking sheet or the grill with cooking spray. Broil, watching carefully, 2 to 3 minutes per side. Let cool.

3. Place a few pepper strips and arugula leaves on top of each zucchini slice. Sprinkle on the cheese if desired. Roll up and secure with a toothpick.

HORSERADISH TUNA ON CUCUMBER ROUNDS

Hollowed-out cucumber rounds make a nice holder for a variety of fillings. One of my favorites is this tangy tuna salad.

MAKES 48

2 cans (7½ ounces each) tuna, drained
½ cup light mayonnaise
4 tablespoons white horseradish
2 tablespoons fresh lemon juice

1 tablespoon finely chopped fresh dill
4 cucumbers, peeled and cut into
  ¾-inch rounds
Fresh dill for garnish

1. Finely chop the tuna in a large bowl. Set aside.

2. Mix the mayonnaise, horseradish, lemon, and dill in a small bowl, and then add to the tuna. Mix well and set aside.

3. Using a melon baller, scoop out the center of each cucumber round, leaving the bottom intact and a ¼-inch border.

4. Using a spoon or the melon baller, fill each cucumber cavity with the tuna mixture. Garnish with a fresh dill sprig if desired. Serve chilled.

An assorted platter of cucumber rounds topped with Horseradish Tuna, Smoked Salmon Spread (page 109), Green Onions, Radish, and Carrot Cream Cheese (page 96), and Vegetable Crabmeat Filling (page 90) is lovely at outdoor spring or summer get-togethers.

Deviled Eggs with Sun-dried Tomato and Roasted Pepper Pesto

Here's another great way to use Sun-dried Tomato and Roasted Pepper Pesto. The contrast between the filling and the hard-cooked egg whites is very appealing.

12 hard-boiled eggs, cut in half
  lengthwise
⅓ cup Sun-dried Tomato and Roasted
  Pepper Pesto (page 85)

Salt and freshly ground pepper to taste
6 oil-packed sun-dried tomatoes,
  drained and cut into thin strips for
  garnish (optional)

1. Remove the yolk from each egg half and place the yolks in a small bowl. Add 4 egg-white halves and finely chop using a metal chopper or fork. Add the pesto and mix evenly. Season with salt and pepper.

2. Pipe or spoon about 1 tablespoon of filling into each egg-white shell. Garnish with sun-dried tomato strips if desired.

Other nice stuffers for egg whites:

- **Basil Pesto Dip (page 34) mixed with egg yolks and egg whites**
- **Green Onions, Radish, and Carrot Cream Cheese (page 96)**
- **Smoked Salmon Spread (page 109)**
- **Black Olivada (page 39) mixed with the egg yolks, egg whites, and a little mayonnaise**

For more traditional eaters, here's an easy recipe for Deviled Eggs:
Combine the yolks of 12 hard-boiled eggs with ¼ cup of mayonnaise, 1 tablespoon of Dijon mustard, and salt and freshly ground pepper to taste. Fill the egg whites with the mixture. Garnish with fresh parsley if desired.

DILLED SHRIMP SALAD ON ENDIVE LEAVES

Endive leaves are a delicious, healthy holder for a variety of fillings.

⅔ pound cooked baby shrimp
¼ cup finely chopped celery
¼ cup finely chopped carrots
¼ cup low-fat mayonnaise
2 tablespoons Dijon mustard

1 tablespoon finely chopped fresh dill
Salt and freshly ground pepper to taste
½ pound Belgian endive, separated
    into leaves
Fresh dill for garnish

1. Place the shrimp, celery, and carrots in a large bowl and set aside.

2. Combine the mayonnaise, mustard, dill, salt, and pepper in a small bowl and mix well.

3. Add the mayonnaise mixture to the shrimp mixture, and mix well to combine.

4. Place a tablespoon of shrimp salad on each endive leaf. Garnish with the fresh dill.

Try some of these fillings:

- **Horseradish Tuna (page 92)**
- **Smoked Salmon Spread (page 109)**
- **Roquefort Ball (page 40)**
- **Sun-dried Tomato and Roasted Pepper Pesto (page 85)**
- **Basil Pesto Dip (page 34)**
- **Green Onions, Radish, and Carrot Cream Cheese (page 96)**
- **Goat Cheese Log with Sun-dried Tomatoes and Basil (page 42)**
- **Vegetable Crabmeat Filling (page 90)**

SMOKED SALMON "FLOWERS"

Chef Sam Fishman, of Sutton Place Gourmet on Long Island, shared this elegant but simple trick for serving smoked salmon. He places the "flowers" on small round crackers with a thin layer of Horseradish Yogurt Sauce (page 77). I also enjoy them with a simple combination of crème fraîche and fresh dill. These will really impress your guests.

MAKES 10

½ *pound smoked salmon, cut into*
  thin slices 3 to 4 inches long and
  2 inches wide

¼ *cup crème fraîche*
2 *tablespoons chopped fresh dill*
10 *small round crackers*

1. Place the smoked salmon on a flat work surface. Fold each piece in half horizontally. Using a sharp knife, cut small slits through the salmon along the folded side, leaving a ¼-inch border on the opposite edges. Beginning at one end, roll up each piece. This will form the flowers.

2. Combine the crème fraîche and dill in a small bowl. Spread a thin layer of dill sauce on each cracker, top with the salmon flowers, and serve.

Fresh Vegetables Stuffed with Green Onions, Radish, and Carrot Cream Cheese

This is an excellent finger food for any occasion, particularly when guests stand while eating. For a more elegant presentation, use a pastry bag with a star tip.

Makes 48

16 medium radishes
16 cherry tomatoes, cut in half
1 cup (8 ounces) light cream cheese
4 green onions, chopped
½ cup shredded carrots

Salt and freshly ground pepper to taste
8 celery stalks, washed, trimmed, and
    halved lengthwise
Chopped parsley for garnish

1. Cut the bottoms of the radishes and tomatoes so they stand upright on a platter. Using a melon baller, cut out the center of each radish and tomato. Discard the tomato pulp. Place the radish centers in a bowl and chop them.

2. Place the cream cheese, onions, carrots, and chopped radishes in a food processor, and blend until combined. Season with salt and pepper.

3. Using a small knife, fill the radishes and celery stalks with the cream cheese mixture. Place a small spoonful of the mixture on the tomato halves. Sprinkle on the parsley for garnish. Serve chilled.

Green Onions, Radish, and Carrot Cream Cheese is also great

- **to spread on bagels**
- **as a filling for omelets**

CHICKEN LIVER PÂTÉ

This spread is excellent with crackers, pita bread rounds, or fresh pear slices.

½ pound whole chicken livers, rinsed, patted dry, and coarsely chopped
Salt and freshly ground pepper to taste
1 tablespoon vegetable oil
1 clove garlic
2 tablespoons finely chopped shallots

2 tablespoons brandy
2 tablespoons butter, softened
2 tablespoons finely chopped shelled skinned pistachio nuts
2 tablespoons dried cranberries
Cornichons for garnish (optional)

1. Season the chicken livers with salt and pepper. In a medium-size pan, heat the oil over medium heat and add the chicken livers and garlic. Cook 2 to 3 minutes, until the chicken livers are golden brown. Add the shallots and cook an additional minute. Remove the pan from heat and discard the garlic. Stir in the brandy and let cool.

2. Place mixture into the bowl of a food processor and process until smooth. Add the butter and process until fully incorporated. Then add nuts and cranberries, reserving enough for garnish if desired, and process using on/off turns until just mixed together. Place the mixture in a bowl and refrigerate until cold. Garnish with dried cranberries and chopped pistachio nuts or sliced cornichons if desired. Serve on crackers, pear slices, or pita bread rounds.

GARLIC AND HERB TOMATOES

My friend David Goldberg whipped these up for our annual holiday party. They disappeared quickly, with rave reviews. I like to serve them on crusty bread or bruschetta.

MAKES 32

16 *plum tomatoes, halved*
½ *cup extra-virgin olive oil*
6 *cloves garlic, minced*
3 *tablespoons finely chopped parsley*

1 *tablespoon finely chopped fresh rosemary or oregano*
Salt and freshly ground pepper to taste
¼ *cup grated Romano cheese*

1. Preheat the oven to 250°F. Place the tomatoes on a large baking sheet.

2. Whisk together the oil, garlic, herbs, salt, and pepper. Drizzle about ½ tablespoon on each tomato half. Let the tomatoes marinate for 30 minutes.

3. Sprinkle the tomatoes with cheese, and bake for 3 hours. Serve warm or at room temperature.

Garlic and Herb Tomatoes are also excellent:

- **Chopped as a topping for focaccia**
- **As a topping for crostini**
- **Chopped as a stuffing for Zucchini Rolls (page 91)**

TRICOLOR TORTELLINI SKEWERS WITH ROASTED PEPPER AND GARLIC DIP

These are beautiful fanned out on an attractive platter. Prepare the dip in advance and soak the skewers in water for 30 minutes. Cook the tortellini and thread on skewers just before guests arrive.

MAKES 30

1 package (1 pound) frozen tricolor
   tortellini
1 tablespoon olive oil
30 small bamboo skewers
7½-ounce jar roasted peppers, drained

2 to 3 cloves garlic, minced
½ teaspoon balsamic vinegar
½ cup light mayonnaise
Salt and freshly ground pepper to taste

1. Heat a large stockpot of salted water to a boil. Add the tortellini and cook until just tender. Drain, and gently toss with the oil. Set aside.

2. Place the peppers and garlic in the bowl of a food processor, and finely chop.

3. Add the vinegar and mayonnaise, and pulse to combine. Season with salt and pepper. Transfer to a small bowl.

4. Thread three tortellini onto each skewer, and serve with the dip.

PLUM TOMATOES WITH MOZZARELLA AND PROSCIUTTO STUFFING

Serve these appetizers with some crusty bread or Garlic Knots (page 26). They are a nice addition to an antipasto platter.

MAKES 24 PIECES

12 plum tomatoes, cored, halved, and
  seeded
⅓ cup olive oil
¾ cup fresh bread crumbs

1 clove garlic, minced
3 ounces thinly sliced prosciutto
½ cup shredded mozzarella cheese
Salt and freshly ground pepper to taste

1. Preheat the oven to 350°F. Heat ¼ cup olive oil in a small pan, and add the bread crumbs, and sauté until golden and crisp. Transfer to a bowl, and add the garlic, prosciutto, cheese, salt, and pepper. Stir to combine.

2. Place about 1 tablespoon of filling in each tomato half. Drizzle with the remaining oil. Place the tomatoes on a baking sheet and bake about 15 minutes, until the cheese is melted and the tomatoes are cooked.

STUFFED EGGPLANT

My friend Robert Martino serves this delicious appetizer with homemade tomato sauce. If you prefer to omit the breading, simply brush a layer of olive oil over the eggplant, bake about 20 minutes until tender, and then fill.

MAKES 10 TO 12 SERVINGS

2 eggplants, cut lengthwise into ¼-inch
   slices
¼ cup milk
2 eggs, lightly beaten
1 cup flavored dried bread crumbs
Vegetable oil for frying

1 cup ricotta cheese
½ cup shredded mozzarella cheese
⅓ cup freshly grated Parmesan cheese
1 clove garlic, minced
Salt and freshly ground pepper to taste
1 cup tomato sauce

1. Preheat the oven to 350°F. Place the eggplant slices in a large bowl. Combine the milk and eggs in a small bowl, and pour over the eggplant. Dredge the eggplant in the bread crumbs. Heat the oil in a large skillet and fry the eggplant 2 to 3 minutes a side, until golden. Drain on paper towels. Let the eggplant cool.

2. Combine the remaining ingredients except the tomato sauce. Place 1 heaping teaspoon of the mixture onto 1 end of each eggplant slice and roll up. Pour a layer of tomato sauce into the baking pan. Place the eggplant rolls on top. Cover with the remaining sauce.

3. Bake 15 to 20 minutes, until the eggplant is hot and the cheese is melted.

**For a slightly different filling, omit the ricotta cheese and
add 3 ounces thinly sliced prosciutto.**

SCALLOPS OREGANATA

My dear friend Julie Morowitz threads her wonderful scallops on miniature skewers for cocktail parties and serves them over pasta for more formal occasions. Either way, they'll be a hit.

1½ pounds small bay scallops
2 to 4 tablespoons olive oil
2 small lemons
2 teaspoons finely chopped garlic

Vegetable oil cooking spray
2 tablespoons seasoned dried bread crumbs

1. Combine the scallops, oil, juice of 1 lemon, and garlic in a small bowl. Gently toss to coat evenly. Refrigerate for 1 to 2 hours.

2. Preheat the broiler. Coat a large skillet with cooking spray and heat over medium heat. Pour in the scallop mixture and sauté over medium-high heat for about 2 minutes, until scallops are opaque.

3. Add the remaining lemon juice to the pan. Sprinkle the scallops with bread crumbs. Place the pan under the broiler and broil about 2 minutes, until tops become lightly brown. Serve immediately.

STUFFED MUSHROOMS

The bacon and Swiss cheese give these mushrooms a unique taste.

MAKES 2 DOZEN

2 tablespoons olive oil
2 dozen white mushrooms, cleaned,
    stems removed and finely chopped,
    caps reserved
½ cup seasoned dried bread crumbs

1 large egg yolk, beaten
¼ cup freshly grated Swiss cheese
4 bacon slices, cooked until crisp and
    crumbled (see page 58)

1. Preheat the oven to 400°F.

2. Heat the oil over medium heat and cook the mushroom stems, stirring for about 5 minutes, until tender.

3. Mix the bread crumbs, egg yolk, cheese, bacon, and sautéed mushrooms together in a small bowl.

4. Mound filling in the reserved mushroom caps. Place in a large shallow baking pan, and bake about 15 minutes, until the mushrooms are brown.

SPINACH AND FETA PUFFS

These flaky puffs have a traditional Greek filling of spinach and Feta cheese. Extra filling would also be good in Fried Won Tons (page 106).

MAKES 18

½ cup crumbled Feta cheese
¼ cup ricotta cheese
¼ cup freshly grated Parmesan cheese
¼ cup frozen chopped spinach, thawed and squeezed dry
¼ teaspoon freshly grated nutmeg

Salt and freshly ground pepper to taste
1 to 2 tablespoons flour
Two-sheet package (17¼ ounces) frozen puff pastry, thawed
Milk

1. Preheat the oven to 400°F. In a medium bowl, combine the Feta, ricotta, 2 table-spoons of the Parmesan, the spinach, nutmeg, salt, and pepper. Set aside.

2. Sprinkle flour on a pastry board and unfold the puff pastry. Cut each sheet into nine 3-inch squares.

3. Place a heaping teaspoon of filling on 1 side of each pastry square. Fold the other side of the pastry over the filling. Seal the package with the tines of a fork. Cut a small slit in the top of each pastry so that air can escape.

4. Brush each pastry with milk, and sprinkle with the remaining Parmesan. Place the pastries 1 or 2 inches apart on a large baking sheet.

5. Bake about 20 minutes, until the pastries are golden. Serve warm.

Fried Ravioli

Serve these with tomato basil sauce. Tortellini will also work nicely in this recipe.

Vegetable oil
1 pound cheese ravioli

Salt to taste
½ cup freshly grated Parmesan cheese

Heat the oil in a large deep pot to 375°F. Fry the ravioli in batches 1 to 2 minutes, until golden. Using a slotted spoon, transfer the ravioli to paper towels, drain, and place them in a bowl. Toss with the salt and Parmesan. Serve with hot tomato sauce for dipping.

FRIED WON TONS

Won ton wrappers make the perfect holder for countless fillings. Guests will find these won tons more exotic than traditional egg rolls and you will find them easier to prepare than expected.

MAKES 30

30 won ton wrappers
1 egg, beaten (optional)
1 batch of Fabulous Won Ton Stuffing
  (page 107)

Vegetable oil for frying

1. Place each won ton wrapper on a flat surface with the point toward you. Place 1 teaspoon of filling in the center of the wrapper. Brush the edges with a little water or a beaten egg. Fold the top point over the filling to form a triangle. Press to seal. Moisten the remaining two bottom points and join together, pressing to seal. Repeat with the remaining won tons.

2. In a heavy large skillet, heat about 2 inches of oil to 350°F. Cook won tons in small batches, turning occasionally, about 1 minute, until crisp and golden. Drain on paper towels, and serve hot.

To make in advance: reheat in a 375°F oven for 15 minutes until hot.

FABULOUS WON TON STUFFING

Stuff the won ton wrappers with any of these wonderful fillings. Then fry as directed on page 106.

SMOKED SALMON FILLING

MAKES 1½ CUPS

Combine ½ cup finely chopped smoked salmon, ½ cup finely chopped red onion, ½ cup sour cream, and 2 tablespoons lemon juice.

SPINACH FLORENTINE FILLING

MAKES 1¼ CUPS

Combine ¾ cup thawed frozen chopped spinach, ½ cup ricotta cheese, 1 minced clove garlic, 1 egg yolk, 1 finely chopped scallion, and salt and freshly ground pepper to taste.

PIZZA FILLING

MAKES 2 CUPS

Combine 1 cup finely shredded mozzarella cheese, ½ cup chopped pepperoni, ⅓ cup tomato sauce, 1 minced clove garlic, and salt and freshly ground pepper to taste.

RASPBERRY CHEESE FILLING

MAKES 2 CUPS

Combine ½ cup farmer cheese, ½ cup cottage cheese, 2 tablespoons cream cheese, ¼ cup sugar, and ¾ cup fresh or frozen chopped raspberries.

SHRIMP AND BACON FILLING

MAKES 1½ CUPS

Combine 1 cup finely chopped cooked shrimp, 5 slices finely crumbled cooked bacon, 2 finely chopped scallions, 1 tablespoon soy sauce, and ¼ teaspoon sesame oil.

TEX-MEX FILLING

MAKES 2 CUPS

Combine 1 cup cooked ground beef with ¼ cup Tomato Salsa (page 28) or your favorite salsa, ½ cup canned refried beans, and ¼ cup shredded cheddar cheese.

A little stuffed won ton is wonderful on its own, but some guests might enjoy a dipping sauce to go with them. Try any of the following combinations:

- **Smoked Salmon won tons or Raspberry Cheese won tons with sour cream**
- **Spinach Florentine won tons with duck sauce**
- **Pizza won tons with tomato sauce**

- **Shrimp and bacon won tons with duck sauce, Chinese plum sauce mixed with a little Dijon mustard, or Soy Dipping Sauce (page 114)**
- **Tex-Mex won tons with salsa**

PUFF PASTRY FILLED WITH SMOKED SALMON SPREAD

Puff pastry rounds make excellent canapés with your favorite filling or spread.

MAKES 50

1 pound frozen puff pastry, thawed   *Smoked Salmon Spread*

1. Preheat the oven to 400°F.

2. Roll out the pastry according to the package directions, and cut into 1-inch circles. Bake about 15 minutes, until puffed and golden. Let cool completely.

3. Cut a slit on one side of each pastry and fill with a heaping teaspoon of the spread.

Some other nice fillings:

- **Herbed cream cheese**
- **Roquefort Ball (page 40)**
- **Whitefish salad**
- **Seafood salad**
- **Dilled Shrimp Salad (page 94)**

SMOKED SALMON SPREAD

MAKES 1½ CUPS

1 package (8 ounces) light cream cheese
3 ounces sliced smoked salmon
1 tablespoon lemon juice
1 tablespoon chopped fresh dill

¼ teaspoon freshly ground black
* pepper*
1½ teaspoons white horseradish

Place all the ingredients in a food processor and process until evenly blended and chopped.

SAUSAGE IN BLANKETS

Add a twist to traditional franks in blankets by substituting your favorite gourmet sausages. My favorite stuffing is chicken, apple, raisin, and sausage. Have a variety of mustards available for dipping.

MAKES ABOUT 30

2 tubes (10 ounces each) refrigerated
    flaky biscuits
2 tablespoons Dijon mustard

¾ pound bulk chicken or turkey sausage
1 egg, beaten

1. Preheat the oven to 400°F.

2. Separate the biscuits and roll flat. Spread a layer of mustard on each circle.

3. Cut the sausage into about 30 pieces, about 1½ inches each. Place a piece on each biscuit. Fold the dough around the sausages, and press the edges together to seal. Place them seam side down on a baking sheet, and brush the dough with the beaten egg.

4. Bake about 15 minutes, until the biscuits are golden and the sausage is done.

If you prefer smaller pieces, cut the biscuits into semicircles and fill with ½-inch pieces of sausage. Seal and bake as directed above.

To make in advance, reheat in a 375°F oven for 10 to 15 minutes until hot.

CRAB FRITTERS

These are a favorite munch in New England. Guests will enjoy the light, flavorful inside and crunchy outside. Serve with Creamy Asian Dipping Sauce, tartar sauce, or Spicy Dipping Sauce (page 76).

MAKES 3 DOZEN

2 eggs, separated
⅔ cup milk
1½ cups flour
½ tablespoon baking powder
1 teaspoon salt
1½ tablespoons hot red pepper sauce

Freshly ground pepper to taste
⅓ cup cream-style corn, drained
4 green onions, finely chopped
2 cans (6 ounces) lump crabmeat,
  picked over, drained and minced
Vegetable oil for frying

1. Using an electric mixer, beat the egg yolks until light.

2. Stir in the milk, flour, baking powder, salt, pepper sauce, and pepper. Mix well.

3. Add the corn, onions, and crabmeat, stirring to combine.

4. Beat the egg whites until stiff. Fold into the fritter mixture.

5. In a large deep pan, heat 1 inch of vegetable oil to 350°F. Drop the batter by table-spoonsful into the hot oil. Cook about 2 minutes, until golden. Drain on paper towels.

> **If you prepare these in advance, recrisp in a 375°F oven for 10 to 15 minutes before serving.**

For variety, you can substitute minced red peppers for the green onions or minced clams for the crabmeat.

CREAMY ASIAN DIPPING SAUCE

⅔ cup mayonnaise

Juice of 1 lime

2 tablespoons finely chopped green
   onions

2 tablespoons sesame oil

1½ tablespoons soy sauce

Combine all ingredients in a small bowl. Serve with the Crab Fritters.

COCKTAIL MEATBALLS

These sweet-and-sour meatballs are so tender they will melt in your mouth. The grape jelly makes a slightly sweeter version than the cranberry sauce.

MAKES 30

¼ cup plain bread crumbs
1 pound ground beef
1 egg
½ teaspoon salt
½ teaspoon garlic powder

1 teaspoon chili powder
1 bottle (12 ounces) chili sauce
1 jar (6 ounces) grape jelly or 1 can
   (16 ounces) whole cranberry sauce

1. Place the bread crumbs, beef, egg, salt, garlic, and chili powder in a large bowl. Mix well to combine. Form into 1-inch meatballs.

2. Place the chili sauce and jelly in a large pot. Heat over medium heat until the jelly is melted. Add the meatballs. Bring to a boil, lower heat to a simmer, and partially cover the pot. Cook about 1 hour, until meatballs are cooked.

BACON-WRAPPED SHRIMP WITH SOY DIPPING SAUCE

These are simple and elegant. Arrange the shrimp on a large platter with a bowl of sauce in the middle for dipping. If you are in a rush, substitute prepared cocktail sauce.

MAKES 34

18 bacon slices, cut in half crosswise
36 uncooked large shrimp, peeled and
    deveined

Soy Dipping Sauce

1. Preheat the broiler.

2. Wrap 1 piece of bacon around each shrimp and secure with a toothpick. Place in a broiler pan. Broil 3 minutes per side, until the bacon is crisp and the shrimp are cooked.

SOY DIPPING SAUCE

MAKES ABOUT ¾ CUP

½ cup soy sauce
2 green onions, thinly sliced
2 tablespoons rice vinegar

2 teaspoons Asian sesame oil
1½ teaspoons finely grated ginger
1 teaspoon sugar

Combine the ingredients together in a small bowl.

Mini Crab Cakes

Serve these with tartar sauce, Creamy Asian Dipping Sauce (page 112) or Spicy Dipping Sauce (page 76).

½ pound fresh (picked over), frozen, or canned lump crabmeat (rinsed and drained)
¼ cup finely chopped celery
¼ cup finely chopped red bell pepper
¼ cup finely chopped Vidalia or red onion
½ cup canned whole-kernel corn

⅓ cup mayonnaise
1 tablespoon Dijon mustard
2 tablespoons finely chopped fresh dill
1 egg, lightly beaten
¾ cup fresh bread crumbs
Salt and freshly ground pepper to taste
Vegetable oil for frying

1. Combine the crabmeat, celery, bell pepper, and onion in a large bowl. Set aside.

2. Mix the mayonnaise, mustard, and dill in a small bowl, and add to the crabmeat mixture.

3. Gently mix in the egg and ⅓ cup of bread crumbs. Season with salt and pepper.

4. Form small patties, about 1 to 2 tablespoons each. Dredge in the remaining bread crumbs. Refrigerate the patties for at least 30 minutes.

5. In a large skillet, heat 2 tablespoons of oil over medium heat. Fry the crab cakes, adding more oil if necessary, about 3 minutes per side, until golden.

SESAME PECAN CHICKEN TENDERS WITH APRICOT DIPPING SAUCE

This recipe is one of my all-time favorites—just about everyone likes these tenders, including the kids. The are delicious hot, cold, or at room temperature and work equally well at formal or casual parties. They even make a great snack!

MAKES 12 CHICKEN TENDERS

2 egg whites
⅓ cup sesame seeds
3 tablespoons finely chopped pecans
Vegetable oil for frying

1 pound skinless, boneless chicken breast, cut into thin strips
Sweet and Spicy Dipping Sauce

1. Beat the egg whites in a small bowl until frothy, and set aside. Combine the sesame seeds and pecans in a small bowl, and set aside.

2. In a large heavy skillet, heat 3 inches of oil over medium heat, until the oil reaches 350°F.

3. Dip the chicken strips into the egg whites and then into the nut mixture. Carefully place a few strips in the hot oil and fry about 3 minutes, until golden brown. Drain on paper towels. Repeat with the remaining strips. Serve with the dipping sauce.

SWEET AND SPICY DIPPING SAUCE

MAKES ABOUT ½ CUP

2 tablespoons hoisin sauce
1 teaspoon Dijon mustard

¼ cup apricot preserves

Combine the hoisin sauce, mustard, and preserves in a small bowl and stir well to combine. Serve with the chicken tenders.

POTATO PANCAKES

These are elegant as an hors d'oeuvre, a light lunch, or a munch. Adding the caviar puts them into a category all their own.

MAKES ABOUT 35

4 medium russet potatoes, peeled and
   cut into chunks
1 medium onion, peeled and cut into
   quarters
1 egg
2 tablespoons flour

1 teaspoon salt
Freshly ground black pepper to taste
Vegetable oil for frying
3½ ounces red, golden, or black caviar
   (optional)
Sour cream (optional)

1. Place the potatoes and onion in a food processor. Process until finely chopped, but not pureed. Alternatively, grate the potatoes and onion with a hand grater. Pour into a bowl.

2. Add the egg, flour, salt, and pepper, stirring to combine.

3. In a large skillet, heat the oil over medium-high heat. Using heaping tablespoons, spoon into the skillet and fry the pancakes about 3 minutes per side, until the filling is cooked and they are golden. Transfer pancakes to paper towels and drain. Top each pancake with a few grains of caviar and a dollop of sour cream if desired.

**For variety, add 1 cup chopped smoked salmon or smoked ham
to the potato batter.**

Something Sweet

Every now and then—and sometimes more than that—you crave something sweet—whether it's a piece of chocolate, a sugary cookie, a blondie, a muffin, a piece of peanut brittle, or an ice cream sundae.

You'll love these sweet treats. Some of them are even low in fat and calories. All are delicious and will satisfy even the sweetest sweet tooth.

CANDY SHOP COOKIES

Try these for an incredible treat—both candy and cookie in every bite.

1 cup flour
½ teaspoon baking soda
¼ teaspoon salt
½ cup unsalted butter, at room
  temperature
⅔ cup firmly packed brown sugar

1 egg
1 teaspoon vanilla
6 ounces Butterfinger Bits or Heath
  Bar Brickle
¾ cup white or semisweet chocolate
  chips

1. Preheat the oven to 375°F.

2. Stir the flour, baking soda, and salt together in a small bowl, and set aside.

3. Using an electric mixer, cream the butter and sugar together.

4. Add the egg and vanilla, and beat well.

5. Stir in the dry ingredients until just combined. Add the candy and chips, and stir to combine.

6. Drop by ¼ cupfuls onto ungreased cookie sheets.

7. Bake about 12 minutes, until set and lightly brown around the edges.

LEMON PIGNOLI CRISPS

Sweet and lemony, these crisp cookies are equally good with your favorite coffee or a scoop of vanilla ice cream. They are even delicious crushed and sprinkled on fruit.

MAKES 30 COOKIES

1½ cups flour
1 teaspoon baking powder
¼ teaspoon salt
½ cup butter, at room temperature
½ cup white sugar
¼ cup firmly packed brown sugar

1 egg
1 tablespoon fresh lemon juice
1 tablespoon grated lemon zest
1 cup pignoli nuts
Vegetable oil cooking spray

1. Combine the flour, baking powder, and salt in a small bowl. Set aside.

2. Using an electric mixer, beat the butter and both sugars together until light and fluffy.

3. Add the egg, lemon juice, and lemon zest and beat well.

4. Gradually add the dry ingredients and blend until just combined. Stir in the pignoli nuts.

5. Coat a 9-inch loaf pan with cooking spray. Press the dough into the pan. Cover with plastic wrap or aluminum foil and freeze about 30 minutes, until firm but not frozen.

6. Preheat the oven to 350°F. Grease a large baking sheet.

7. Remove the dough from the pan by cutting around the edge with a spatula and lifting up. Slice the dough widthwise into slices that are about ¼ inch thick. Place on the prepared sheet.

8. Bake 12 to 14 minutes, until set and edges are slightly brown.

NUTTY THUMBPRINT COOKIES

The sweet nuttiness of these cookies is an excellent accompaniment to a cup of strong coffee.

MAKES 24 COOKIES

Vegetable oil cooking spray
1 cup flour
¼ teaspoon baking soda
¼ teaspoon salt
½ cup butter, at room temperature
⅓ cup firmly packed brown sugar
1 egg

1 teaspoon vanilla
¾ cup, coarsely ground macadamia
    nuts
⅓ cup white sugar
Approximately 3 tablespoons of
    raspberry or strawberry jam

1. Preheat the oven to 350°F. Coat a large baking sheet with cooking spray.

2. Combine the flour, baking soda, and salt in a small bowl, and set aside.

3. Using an electric mixer, cream the butter and brown sugar until light and fluffy. Add the egg and vanilla, and beat well.

4. Gradually blend in the flour mixture, until just combined. Stir in the nuts.

5. Roll pieces of the dough into 1-inch balls. Roll each ball in the white sugar. Place on the prepared baking sheet, 2 inches apart. Using your thumb, make an indentation about ¼ inch deep in the center of each cookie.

6. Bake for 10 minutes. Fill each indentation with ¼ teaspoon jam. Bake about 10 minutes more, until the cookies turn golden. Cool completely on wire racks.

CHOCOLATE HAZELNUT THINS

These long, thin crisps are a coffee bar staple. They are also delicious with a glass of cold milk.

MAKES 30 COOKIES

1½ cups flour
1 teaspoon baking powder
⅓ cup unsweetened cocoa
1 teaspoon ground cinnamon
¼ teaspoon salt
½ cup unsalted butter, at room
  temperature

¾ cup sugar
1 egg
1 teaspoon vanilla extract
¾ cup chopped hazelnuts
Vegetable oil cooking spray

1. Combine the flour, baking powder, cocoa, cinnamon, and salt in a small bowl, and set aside.

2. Using an electric mixer, beat the butter and sugar until light and fluffy. Add the egg and vanilla, and beat well.

3. Gradually add the dry ingredients until just combined. Stir in the nuts.

4. Coat a 9-inch loaf pan with cooking spray. Press the dough into the pan. Cover with plastic wrap or aluminum foil and freeze for 20 minutes, until firm.

5. Preheat the oven to 350°F. Grease a large baking sheet.

6. Remove the dough from the pan by cutting around the edge with a spatula and lifting up. Slice the dough widthwise into slices that are about ¼ inch thick. Place on prepared sheet.

7. Bake for 12 to 14 minutes, until set and edges are slightly brown.

CEREAL COOKIES

If you like sugar-coated corn flakes cereal, you'll flip over these cookies.

MAKES 2 DOZEN

Vegetable oil cooking spray
1 cup flour
½ teaspoon baking powder
½ teaspoon baking soda
¾ cup sugar

½ cup shortening
½ teaspoon vanilla
1 egg
2¼ cups sugar-coated corn flakes cereal
1 cup raisins

1. Preheat the oven to 350°F. Spray baking sheets with cooking spray.

2. Combine the flour, baking powder, and baking soda in a small bowl, and set aside.

3. Cream the sugar and shortening together until light. Add the vanilla and egg, and beat well. Stir in the flour mixture and then the cereal.

4. Drop by rounded tablespoonsful onto prepared sheets. Bake for 10 to 12 minutes, until set. Cool completely on wire racks.

RAISIN NUT TWISTS

These twists are light, sweet, and delicious—plus they are a cinch to make with the help of frozen puff pastry. Excellent with coffee or espresso.

MAKES 15

Vegetable oil cooking spray
1 frozen puff pastry sheet, thawed
2 tablespoons raspberry jam

½ cup raisins, coarsely chopped
½ cup almonds, finely ground

1. Preheat the oven to 400°F. Coat a large cookie sheet with cooking spray.

2. Unroll the pastry into a 10- by 10-inch square. Spread the jam evenly over the pastry. Cut the pastry in half.

3. Sprinkle the raisins and nuts over one half of the pastry. Top with the remaining pastry, jam side down. Lightly roll to seal.

4. Cut the pastry into 15 strips. Twist each strip and place on a cookie sheet. Bake about 10 minutes, until golden.

CRANBERRY ORANGE SCONES

These are lovely with sweet butter, orange marmalade, and fresh berries. You can substitute dried cherries or currants, if you prefer.

Vegetable oil cooking spray
1 cup plus 1 tablespoon flour
1 tablespoon sugar
2½ teaspoons baking powder
2 tablespoons sweet butter, cut into
  small pieces

1 egg, beaten
¼ cup heavy cream
1 tablespoon finely grated orange zest
½ cup dried cranberries

1. Preheat the oven to 425°F. Spray a baking sheet with cooking spray.

2. Combine 1 cup flour, the sugar, and baking powder in a medium-size bowl. Using a pastry blender or 2 knives, cut in the butter until it resembles coarse meal. Stir in the egg, cream, and orange zest, and mix until just combined. Gently stir in the cranberries. Gather the dough into a ball.

3. Sprinkle the remaining flour on a pastry board and roll the dough to a thickness of ½ inch. Using a large round glass or a 4-inch cookie cutter, cut out 4 circles. Place on the prepared sheet.

4. Bake for 15 to 17 minutes, until scones just begin to brown.

Create your own scones by omitting the orange zest and cranberries and substituting your favorite fillings. Here are some ideas:

- Chopped nuts and lemon zest
- Chocolate chips and dried cherries
- Raisins or dates and chopped walnuts

Banana Chip Muffins

These are wonderful with coffee or hot chocolate. Try them for breakfast, brunch, or snacktime. They even make a nice lunchbox treat or after-school snack.

MAKES 12

Vegetable oil cooking spray
1½ cups whole-wheat flour
1½ teaspoons baking soda
¼ teaspoon salt
2 large ripe bananas, mashed
½ cup white sugar
¼ cup firmly packed brown sugar

½ cup butter, melted
½ cup milk
1 egg
½ cup semisweet chocolate chips
½ cup pecans, walnuts, or macadamia nuts, chopped (optional)

1. Preheat the oven to 350°F. Spray a 12-cup muffin tin with cooking spray.

2. Stir the flour, baking soda, and salt together in a small bowl, and set aside.

3. Mix the bananas, both sugars, butter, milk, and egg together in a large bowl.

4. Add the flour mixture, and blend until just combined. Fold in the chocolate chips and nuts if desired. Fill prepared muffin cups ⅔ full.

5. Bake at 350°F for 25 minutes. Cool completely on a wire rack.

DATE AND NUT BARS

You'll enjoy these with a tall glass of Lemonade (page 161) or Flavored Iced Tea (page 163).

MAKES 30

Vegetable oil cooking spray
¾ cup flour
½ teaspoon baking powder
2 eggs
1 cup sugar

½ cup vegetable oil
1½ cups chopped dates
1½ cups chopped pecans or almonds
Powdered sugar for topping (optional)

1. Preheat the oven to 350°F. Spray a 9- by 13-inch baking pan with cooking spray.

2. Combine the flour and baking powder in a small bowl, and set aside.

3. Whisk together the eggs, sugar, and oil. Add the flour mixture, and mix well.

4. Stir in the dates and nuts.

5. Press the mixture into the prepared pan. Bake about 45 minutes, until golden.

6. Cut into squares while hot. Let cool completely. Sprinkle with powdered sugar if desired.

HAZELNUT BLONDIES

Ground vanilla wafer cookies give these easy-to-make sweets an interesting taste and texture.

Vegetable oil cooking spray
2 cups coarsely ground vanilla wafer
  cookies
1 can (14 ounces) sweetened
  condensed milk

⅔ cup chopped hazelnuts
¾ cup white chocolate chips

1. Preheat the oven to 350°F. Spray an 8-inch-square pan with cooking spray.

2. Combine the ground cookies, milk, and chocolate chips in a large bowl. Pour into the baking pan and spread evenly.

3. Bake about 30 minutes, until light brown and set. Cool completely and cut into small squares.

For Heath Bar Blondies, substitute 1 cup Heath Bar Brickle or chopped English Toffee for the hazelnuts.

GINGERBREAD

This comforting, flavorful treat is fabulous with lemonade, fruit drinks, tea, or your favorite coffee. Serve with a scoop of vanilla or pumpkin ice cream for a lovely dessert.

Vegetable oil cooking spray
2 cups whole-wheat flour
½ teaspoon baking soda
¾ teaspoon baking powder
½ teaspoon salt
1¼ teaspoons ground ginger

1 teaspoon ground cinnamon
2 eggs, lightly beaten
½ cup dark molasses
¾ cup firmly packed dark brown sugar
½ cup vegetable oil
½ cup boiling water

1. Preheat the oven to 350°F. Spray a 9-inch-square pan with cooking spray.

2. Sift the flour, baking soda, baking powder, salt, ginger, and cinnamon together in a large bowl.

3. Add the eggs, molasses, and sugar, and mix well. Pour on the oil and boiling water. Mix well.

4. Pour into prepared pan. Bake for 35 to 40 minutes, until a tester inserted in the center comes out clean. Let the gingerbread cool completely.

ICING

Here's a simple icing that adds a nice touch to the gingerbread.

MAKES 1 CUP

¼ cup softened butter
½ cup (4 ounces) softened cream cheese
1½ cups confectioners' sugar

1 teaspoon vanilla
¼ teaspoon ground ginger or pumpkin
*   pie spice*

Beat together the butter, cream cheese, and sugar until smooth. Stir in the vanilla and the ginger or pumpkin pie spice. Spread icing with a spatula.

LIGHT MINI CHEESECAKES

These delicious individual cheesecakes are perfect when you want to indulge with a little less guilt.

1 package (8 ounces) light cream
   cheese, at room temperature
½ can fat-free sweetened condensed
   milk

3 tablespoons fresh lemon juice
1 teaspoon grated lemon zest
6 reduced-fat chocolate sandwich
   cookies

1. Using an electric mixer at medium speed, whip the cream cheese for about 5 minutes.

2. Add the condensed milk, lemon juice, and lemon zest. Beat for an additional 2 minutes.

3. Line a muffin pan with foil cups, place a cookie in each one, and fill with the batter. Refrigerate until set.

STRAWBERRY SHORTCAKES

These are perfect in the early summer, when strawberries are at their peak. Some café au lait or café vanilla would make a good accompaniment. For dessert, the shortcakes are great with ice cream; by themselves, they make a delicious breakfast.

MAKES 4 SERVINGS

4 cups thinly sliced hulled strawberries
¼ cup sugar
1 tablespoon fresh lemon juice
4 small plain, strawberry, or blueberry
* scones, split in half*

1 pint strawberry ice cream or sorbet,
* slightly softened (optional)*
Whipped cream, for garnish

1. Combine the strawberries, sugar, and lemon juice in a small bowl. Let stand at room temperature for about 30 minutes, stirring occasionally.

2. Place the bottoms of the scones in deep individual serving bowls. Top with a scoop of ice cream if desired.

3. Spoon strawberries and strawberry juice over the ice cream. Cover with tops of scones. Garnish with the whipped cream.

EASY FRUIT COBBLER

You can substitute apples, peaches, pears, strawberries, or your favorite pourable fruit preserves, to create a variety of cobblers. Add a dollop of whipped cream or some vanilla frozen yogurt for an extra-special treat. This is a perfect evening snack— slightly sweet, satisfying, and light.

MAKES 4 TO 6 SERVINGS

1½ cups blueberries
1 cup raspberries or strawberries
2 tablespoons raspberry pourable fruit
    preserves

¼ cup sugar
1 cup Granola (page 49) or low-fat
    granola cereal
Lemon sorbet (optional)

1. Preheat the oven to 400°F.

2. Combine the blueberries, strawberries, pourable fruit, and sugar in a 2-quart casserole.

3. Bake for 20 minutes, stirring occasionally. Sprinkle on granola and bake for an additional 10 minutes, until granola is brown. Serve with a scoop of lemon sorbet if desired.

Baked Apples with Dried Cranberries and Granola

The granola coating adds a special touch to this homey snack.

MAKES 4

4 large tart apples
¼ cup orange juice or apple cider
¼ cup dried cranberries
½ cup firmly packed brown sugar

½ cup Granola (page 49) or granola
  cereal, finely ground
2½ tablespoons butter

1. Preheat the oven to 350°F. Core the apples, leaving the bottoms intact. Peel about ½ of the skin, starting from the top. Leave the remaining skin intact. Place in a shallow baking pan and pour about 1 inch of orange juice or cider into the pan.

2. Combine the cranberries, sugar, and granola in a small bowl. Fill the cored apples with the mixture, and dot the filling with butter.

3. Bake for 35 to 45 minutes, until tender. Baste with the pan juices.

Ice Cream Cookiewiches

These are simple to prepare, but do need a few hours in the freezer. Make some extra—that way, when the urge hits, these treats will be waiting for you.

MAKES 4

1 pint vanilla ice cream, softened
8 white chocolate chunk cookies
½ cup white chocolate chips

½ cup chopped roasted macadamia nuts

1. Line a cookie sheet with foil.

2. Sandwich ⅓ cup of the ice cream between 2 cookies. Press lightly until the ice cream reaches the edge of the sandwich. Repeat with remaining cookies and ice cream.

3. Combine the chips and nuts in a small bowl. Roll sides of sandwiches in the chip mixture. Press lightly to adhere. Freeze on cookie sheet until firm, at least 15 minutes.

4. Wrap in individual freezer bags. Let stand a few minutes at room temperature before serving if solidly frozen.

To make a light version, sandwich fat-free sorbet between mini chocolate-covered or caramel rice cakes.

INDIVIDUAL BLACK-AND-WHITE ICE CREAM PIES

When you feel like treating yourself or others to something extra special, try this simple snack.

MAKES 8 SERVINGS

28 chocolate sandwich cookies,
   broken into pieces
¼ cup unsalted butter, melted
1 quart vanilla ice cream, slightly
   softened

1 cup white chocolate chips
½ cup prepared fudge sauce

1. Place the cookies in a food processor and finely grind. Set aside ½ cup. Add the butter to the remaining crumbs and process until crumbs begin to clump together. Press into 8 individual tart pans. Freeze for 15 minutes.

2. Meanwhile, mix the ice cream and chocolate chips together. Spoon the mixture into pies. Freeze for 30 minutes.

3. Drizzle on the fudge sauce and sprinkle with the remaining cookie crumbs. Freeze about 30 minutes, until firm.

In a rush?

- Purchase a ready-to-eat chocolate cookie pie crust and make one big ice cream pie.

- Use chocolate-chip ice cream instead of vanilla ice cream and chocolate chips.

For a lighter version, substitute fat-free chocolate cookie wafers, light margarine, and sorbet.

LOW-FAT FROZEN COOKIE PUDDING

It may sound strange, but it sure hits the spot—this pudding is cold, satisfying, and delicious without a lot of calories or fat.

1½ cups cold skim milk
1 package (4-serving-size) chocolate sugar-free instant pudding and pie filling

3¼ cups light frozen whipped topping, thawed
1 cup crushed fat-free chocolate wafer or graham cracker cookies

1. Whisk the milk and pudding together in a large bowl for about 2 minutes, or until thick.

2. Gently stir in the whipped topping and cookies.

3. Pour into a plastic freezer container and freeze at least six hours. Let it sit at room temperature for a few minutes before serving if solidly frozen.

LOW-FAT CHOCOLATE YOGURT POPS

These are like a Fudgsicle, but much lower in fat and calories. You can eat one every day—guilt-free! Plus, these are much less expensive than store-bought pops and take only minutes to prepare.

MAKES 10 POPSICLES

1 cup raspberry fruit juice
3 tablespoons confectioners' sugar

1 container (8 ounces) low-fat
  chocolate yogurt

Combine the ingredients in a small bowl. Spoon into 10 frozen pop molds or 10 paper cups with wooden Popsicle sticks inserted. Freeze until firm.

For variety, omit the raspberry juice and chocolate yogurt. Substitute:

- **For strawberry pops: mixed berry fruit juice and strawberry yogurt**
- **For lemon pops: lemonade and lemon yogurt**
- **For pineapple pops: pineapple juice and pineapple yogurt**
- **For your favorite pops: 1 cup fruit juice and 1 cup yogurt of your choice**

TROPICAL FRUIT SPLIT

Here is an interesting twist on a traditional favorite.

1 small pineapple, peeled, cored and
    cut into ½-inch-thick slices
⅓ cup firmly packed brown sugar
½ teaspoon ground cinnamon
¼ cup butter
2 pints fruit sorbet or vanilla frozen
    yogurt

½ cup raspberry or strawberry fruit
    syrup
¾ cup shredded sweetened coconut or
    Granola (page 49) (optional)

1. Preheat the oven to 400°F.

2. Arrange the pineapple in a baking dish. Sprinkle on the sugar and cinnamon. Dot with butter. Bake about 25 minutes, until bubbly.

3. Divide the pineapple and arrange in 4 sundae dishes. Top with the sorbet, syrup, and coconut or granola if desired.

CHOCOLATE PEANUT BUTTER CANDY SQUARES

One square will satisfy your sweet tooth, but you'll probably want more!

MAKES 36 SQUARES

Vegetable oil cooking spray
1 cup (8 ounces) peanut butter chips
2 cups (16 ounces) milk chocolate chips

½ cup butter
¾ cup chopped pecans
1 cup Heath Bar Brickle

1. Spray a 9- by 13-inch pan with cooking spray.

2. Place the peanut butter chips, milk chocolate chips, and butter in a bowl and set over another saucepan of barely simmering water. Heat, stirring frequently, until smooth and melted. Let the mixture cool slightly.

3. Add the remaining ingredients, spread into the prepared pan, and refrigerate until set. Cut into small squares.

Try some of these combinations:

- **White chocolate chips, raisins, nuts, and dried fruit**
- **Milk chocolate chips, pecans, coconut, and marshmallows**
- **Milk chocolate chips, rice cereal, and marshmallows**
- **Semisweet chocolate, raisins, and peanuts**

CHOCOLATE TRUFFLES WITH KAHLÚA AND PECANS

These elegant chocolates are a perfect accompaniment to your favorite coffee or espresso. A little cognac would also be a nice touch.

MAKES 25

¾ cup whipping cream
1½ cups (12 ounces) semisweet
   chocolate bars, finely chopped

2 tablespoons Kahlúa
1¼ cups finely chopped pecans

1. Line an 8-inch-square baking pan with foil. Set aside.

2. Bring the cream to a simmer, remove from the heat, and whisk in the chocolate until smooth and melted.

3. Whisk in the Kahlúa. Pour the mixture into the prepared pan and freeze about 30 minutes, until just firm.

4. Cut the chocolate into 25 squares. Pour the nuts into a small bowl. Coat each square with nuts and roll into a ball.

5. Place the chocolates on a small baking sheet and chill until firm, at least 2 hours. Serve cold.

Try some of these combinations:

- **Substitute Grand Marnier for the Kahlúa.**
- **Substitute almonds or hazelnuts for the pecans.**

TRAIL MIX CLUSTERS

This snack is sweet and packed with lots of energy-boosting ingredients.

1 package (6 ounces) butterscotch chips
⅓ cup peanut butter
1 cup trail mix

2 cups low-fat granola cereal or
    Granola (page 49)

1. Place the butterscotch chips in a small bowl and set over another saucepan of barely simmering water. Heat, stirring frequently, until smooth and melted.

2. Stir in the peanut butter until smooth.

3. Add the remaining ingredients and stir to coat evenly.

4. Form clusters with a tablespoon and place on wax paper. Let harden before serving.

CHOCOLATE COOKIE BARS

These are an irresistible snack for chocolate lovers. Team with a cup of strong Café Mocha (page 154).

MAKES APPROXIMATELY 20 BARS

1 cup crumbled almond biscotti, Lemon Pignoli Crisps (page 121), or Chocolate Hazelnut Thins (page 123)

10 ounces good-quality white, milk, or dark chocolate chips, melted (see page 149)

1. Stir the biscotti crumbs into the melted chocolate.

2. Spread the chocolate mixture onto a baking sheet lined with wax paper to a thickness of ½ inch. Using a dull knife, make lines across the chocolate mixture, about 2 inches apart for later cutting. Refrigerate at least 1 hour.

3. Cut the chocolate apart with a sharp knife, using the lines as a guide. Break into smaller pieces if desired.

Try these variations.

For toffee cookie bars: Mix ½ cup chopped English toffee into the biscotti crumbs. Stir into the melted chocolate. Follow steps 2 and 3.

For black-and-white cookie bars: Use Chocolate Hazelnut Thins (page 123) and white chocolate.

DOUBLE PEANUT BRITTLE

The addition of peanut butter chips puts this brittle over the top.

½ cup butter, at room temperature
1 cup coarsely chopped unsalted
   peanuts

½ cup sugar
1 tablespoon light corn syrup
¾ cup peanut butter chips

1. Line the bottom and sides of an 8-inch-square baking pan with aluminum foil. Lightly butter the foil.

2. Place the nuts, butter, sugar, and corn syrup in a heavy nonstick saucepan. Cook over low heat, stirring, until the butter melts and sugar dissolves. Raise the heat and boil mixture, stirring constantly, about 3 minutes, until it turns golden brown and begins to clump together.

3. Pour the mixture into the prepared pan and spread evenly. Quickly sprinkle on the peanut butter chips. Spread the melting chips evenly over the brittle, and let cool for 10 minutes.

4. Refrigerate about 20 more minutes, until the melted chips are set. Using the foil, remove the candy from the pan. Peel the foil and break into pieces.

WHITE CHOCOLATE RAISIN NUT BARK

A small piece is an excellent after-dinner snack with a cup of strong coffee.

MAKES ABOUT 3 DOZEN

10 to 20 graham cracker squares
½ cup chopped white chocolate chips
¼ cup raisins

¼ cup roasted peanuts, chopped
¼ cup candy-coated chocolate pieces,
such as M&Ms

1. Cover the bottom of an 8-inch-square baking pan with graham crackers. Place the white chocolate chips in a small bowl and set over another saucepan of barely simmering water. Heat, stirring frequently, until smooth and melted.

2. Spread the melted chips over the graham crackers.

3. Combine the raisins, nuts, and candy in a small bowl. Sprinkle over the melted chocolate. Press lightly to adhere.

4. Place the baking dish in the refrigerator at least 1 hour, until firm. Break bark into pieces. Store in airtight containers.

For peanut butter chocolate bark, substitute peanut butter chips for the white chocolate chips. Spread melted chips on the graham crackers and sprinkle on 1 cup of mini chocolate chips.

WHITE CHOCOLATE–COVERED DRIED FRUIT

Just a few of these sweet, chewy treats will hit the spot. They are a terrific snack while playing board games or cards—no mess. They also go nicely on a platter of assorted sweets.

MAKES 2 CUPS

1 cup white chocolate chips
2 cups mixed dried fruit (apple slices, pineapple, apricots, or pears)

½ cup finely chopped Granola (page 49), or finely chopped nuts

1. Cover a baking sheet with wax paper.

2. Melt the chocolate. Cover half of each piece of dried fruit with chocolate by holding one end and dipping the other half in. Quickly dip into the Granola or nuts and place on the prepared baking sheet. Refrigerate until set.

> To melt chocolate, place the chocolate in a small bowl and set over another saucepan of barely simmering water. Heat the chocolate, stirring frequently, until smooth and melted.

BERRY DIP

Serve this light, fruity sauce with a platter of assorted melons, plums, pears, and peaches cut into bite-size pieces. Cubes of angel food cake or fat-free pound cake are also delicious.

*8 ounces fresh or thawed frozen
   strawberries or blueberries*
½ cup nonfat cottage cheese

¼ cup light sour cream
2 tablespoons sugar
1 tablespoon fresh lemon juice

1. Place the berries and cottage cheese in a food processor and process until smooth, about 2 minutes.

2. Stir in the remaining ingredients and serve cold.

CHOCOLATE SAUCE

I like to offer two sauces with a fruit platter. Berry Dip (page 150) and this Chocolate Sauce make an excellent combination of elegance and decadence.

MAKES ABOUT 1 CUP

1 cup corn syrup
¾ cup heavy cream
1½ cups semisweet chocolate chips,
  chopped

3 tablespoons raspberry or hazelnut
  syrup

1. Place the corn syrup and cream in a small saucepan and bring to a boil. Remove from the heat and stir in the chocolate until smooth.

2. Stir in the raspberry or hazelnut syrup and serve warm. The sauce can be reheated in the microwave until desired temperature, 30 seconds to 1 minute.

Something to Drink

Exotic fresh juices, smoothies, shakes, sodas, coffees, and teas have evolved from a morning fix or after-dinner drink into a gourmet treat. Coffee and juice bars serve these wonderful drinks with muffins, cookies, cakes, sandwiches, salads, and chocolates.

With a good coffee and espresso maker, a juicer, and a blender, you can make these drinks in your home, at your own convenience, and at a fraction of the cost of take-out. They are a wonderful snack all on their own or can be teamed with any of the delicious "little somethings" throughout the book.

> **If you have the space, keep the espresso maker or juicer out on your kitchen counter. Let's face it—once it's stored in a cabinet, we usually forget about it.**

BREWED COFFEE SPECIALTIES

You'll need a home espresso machine with a built-in steamer to make the steamed milk and foam—it's worth the investment, and just a little fruit, nut, or spice flavored syrup will add a burst of flavor to your favorite drink. These excellent natural flavorings are available at specialty food stores and some coffee bars. Simply pour about ½ ounce of syrup into your favorite coffee drink and indulge your taste buds. Now, relax . . . and take a coffee break.

MAKES 1 CUP

Café au Lait
½ cup hot brewed coffee
½ cup steamed milk, plus a layer of foam

A sprinkle of ground cinnamon, nutmeg, or cocoa powder (optional)

Pour the coffee into a mug. Add the steamed milk to the coffee; gently add a layer of foam. Sprinkle on cinnamon, nutmeg, or cocoa powder if desired.

Café Mocha
1 tablespoon chocolate syrup
½ cup hot brewed coffee
½ cup steamed milk, plus a layer of foam

A sprinkle of ground cinnamon, nutmeg, or cocoa powder (optional)

Coat the bottom of a mug with the chocolate syrup, and pour the coffee into the mug. Add the steamed milk to the coffee; gently add a layer of foam. Sprinkle on cinnamon, nutmeg, or cocoa powder if desired.

Café Vanilla

¼ *cup hot brewed coffee*

¼ *teaspoon vanilla-flavored syrup*

¼ *cup steamed milk, plus a layer of*
   foam

A sprinkle of ground cinnamon,
   nutmeg, or cocoa powder (optional)

Pour the coffee into a mug and stir in the syrup. Add the steamed milk to the coffee; gently add a layer of foam. Sprinkle on cinnamon, nutmeg, or cocoa powder if desired.

Café con Panna

1 cup strong, hot brewed coffee

A dollop of whipped cream

A sprinkle of ground cinnamon or
   nutmeg (optional)

Pour the coffee into a mug, top with the whipped cream, and sprinkle with cinnamon or nutmeg if desired.

Espresso Specialties

Although the variations among these strong coffee drinks seem slight, the flavors are different. Once you acquire a taste, you'll be hooked!

Espresso Romano
1½ ounces espresso
Peel of 1 small lemon

Pour the espresso into a 3-ounce cup and garnish with the lemon peel.

Cappuccino
1½ ounces espresso
1½ ounces steamed milk
1½ ounces foam
A sprinkle of ground cinnamon, nutmeg, or sweetened cocoa powder (optional)

Pour the espresso into a 6-ounce cup. Add the steamed milk and foam. Garnish with cinnamon, nutmeg, or cocoa powder if desired.

Mochaccino
1½ ounces espresso
1 tablespoon chocolate syrup
1½ ounces steamed milk
1½ ounces foam
A sprinkle of sweetened cocoa powder (optional)

Pour the espresso into a 6-ounce cup. Stir in the syrup, and add the steamed milk and foam. Garnish with cocoa powder if desired.

Café Latte

1½ ounces espresso

3 ounces steamed milk, plus a layer of foam

A sprinkle of ground cinnamon, nutmeg, or sweetened cocoa powder (optional)

Pour the espresso into a 6-ounce cup. Add the steamed milk and foam. Garnish with cinnamon, nutmeg, or cocoa powder if desired.

Mocha Latte

1½ ounces espresso

1 tablespoon chocolate syrup

3 ounces steamed milk, plus a layer of foam

A sprinkle of ground cinnamon, nutmeg, or sweetened cocoa powder (optional)

Pour the espresso into a 6-ounce cup. Stir in the syrup. Add the steamed milk and a layer of foam. Garnish with cinnamon, nutmeg, or cocoa powder if desired.

FROZEN COFFEE SMOOTHIES

These frosty drinks are a wonderful substitute for hot coffee during the summer months. You can omit the ice cream and add a little extra ice for a simple iced espresso.

Coffee Smoothie

1 cup cold strong coffee

1 container (8 ounces) nonfat vanilla
  yogurt

2½ tablespoons sugar

¼ teaspoon ground cinnamon

1 tablespoon chocolate syrup
  (optional)

1 cup crushed ice

Hazelnut Espresso Smoothie

1 teaspoon hazelnut Italian syrup

½ cup cold espresso

½ cup cold milk

1 scoop vanilla ice cream

1 cup crushed ice

1. Place all the ingredients except the ice in a blender. Blend until smooth.

2. Place the crushed ice into 2 glasses, and pour over coffee mixture.

To add some zip:

- **Pour in some club soda.**
- **Stir in 1 to 2 teaspoons of Italian syrup.**

- **Pour in ¼ cup coffee liqueur.**

HOT CHOCOLATE

The perfect way to warm up on a cold winter's day is to sit near the fireplace, snuggle with an afghan, and sip away the cold with a soothing hot chocolate. Serve this with Banana Chip Muffins (page 128) or Hazelnut Blondies (page 130) for a great treat after playing in the snow.

MAKES 4 SERVINGS

1 quart milk
⅓ cup unsweetened cocoa
¼ cup sugar

1 to 2 tablespoons amaretto, hazelnut, or raspberry syrup (optional)

1. Pour the milk into a saucepan and heat.

2. Mix the cocoa and sugar together in a small bowl. Add about ½ cup of the hot milk, making sure the cocoa mixture is dissolved, then add to the remaining milk. Add flavored syrup if desired.

3. Heat, stirring constantly, until the mixture is very hot. Pour into mugs.

HOT APPLE CIDER

This is terrific on a brisk autumn day, at a Halloween party, or during a cozy evening by the fire. Feel free to spike the cider with apple brandy.

1 gallon apple cider
1 small orange

1 teaspoon whole cloves
4 cinnamon sticks, broken in half

1. Stud the orange with the cloves.

2. Place all the ingredients into a medium saucepan and bring to a boil. Reduce heat to low and simmer for 5 minutes. Discard the orange. Ladle into mugs.

For hot buttered cider, add a tablespoon of melted butter to each serving.

LEMONADE

This is a fantastic thirst quencher anytime. Lemonade is wonderful accompanied by Nutty Thumbprint Cookies (page 122), Chocolate Hazelnut Thins (page 123), or a piece of Gingerbread (page 131).

MAKES 2 QUARTS

Lemonade

6 cups water

1 cup sugar

4 lemons, juiced

Ice

1 fresh mint sprig

Berry Lemonade

6 cups water

1 cup sugar

4 lemons, juiced

1 cup pureed and strained mixed
   berries, such as raspberries,
strawberries, and blueberries, or
¼ cup raspberry syrup (available
   at specialty food stores)
Ice
Fresh mint sprigs for garnish (optional)

Lemon Limeade

6 cups water

1 cup sugar

2 lemons, juiced

3 limes, juiced

Ice

Fresh mint sprigs

1. Place 1 cup of the water and the sugar in a small saucepan. Bring to a boil over high heat and cook for 2 minutes. Let cool.

2. Combine the sugar syrup with the fruit juice and the remaining water; stir well. Refrigerate until cold. Serve over ice, garnished with the mint.

GOOD OL'-FASHIONED EGG CREAM

This is an old-time favorite. Try some of the unusual variations when you want something a little more exotic. Either way, an egg cream will bring out the little kid in you.

Ol'-fashioned Egg Cream
2 tablespoons chocolate syrup
2 ounces cold milk or half-and-half
Cold seltzer

Hazelnut Egg Cream
2 tablespoons hazelnut syrup
2 ounces cold milk or half-and-half
Cold seltzer

Coffee Egg Cream
1 tablespoon chocolate syrup
2 tablespoons cold strong coffee
¼ cup (2 ounces) cold milk or
    half-and-half
Cold seltzer

Place the syrup and coffee, if using, in a tall glass, and stir in the milk or half-and-half. Pour in the seltzer, stirring well to form a large head at the top.

Create unique egg creams by using your favorite Italian fruit or nut syrup, milk, and seltzer. Garnish with a little ice cream or whipped cream if desired.

FLAVORED ICED TEA

Iced tea has become a popular drink year round. Try making your own—it's easy, delicious, and a lot cheaper than bottled brands.

1 quart water
2 plain or flavored tea bags
¼ cup fruit or nut syrup (available in some supermarkets and specialty food stores)

Sugar to taste
Ice cubes
Fresh mint sprigs for garnish (optional)

1. Boil the water. Pour into a pitcher.

2. Add the tea bags. Stir in the syrup. Let cool, and remove the tea bags. Add sugar if desired.

3. Fill tall glasses with ice, and pour in tea. Garnish with mint if desired.

Try these fabulous iced tea combinations:

- **Cinnamon tea with hazelnut syrup**
- **Raspberry tea with raspberry syrup and fresh mint**
- **Black tea with orange syrup and a lemon slice**
- **Strawberry tea with strawberry syrup and fresh mint**

ISLAND DELIGHTS

Relax, sip, and enjoy. Add some light rum or a scoop of vanilla ice cream if you like. These drinks are excellent with nachos, flavored nuts, potato skins, guacamole, black bean dip, chips, and, of course, your favorite something.

Strawberry Banana Colada

1 banana
⅓ cup frozen strawberries
2 tablespoons canned cream of coconut
¼ cup pineapple juice
½ cup ice

Island Paradise

½ cup frozen sweetened strawberries
2 tablespoons canned cream of coconut
¼ cup orange juice
¼ cup pineapple juice
½ cup ice

Piña Colada

¼ cup canned cream of coconut
½ cup pineapple juice
½ cup ice

Strawberry Daiquiri

½ cup frozen sweetened strawberries
¼ cup sweet-and-sour mix
½ cup ice

Place all ingredients in a blender and blend until smooth. Garnish with fresh fruit slices or wedges if desired.

FROZEN FRUIT SHAKES

Thick, delicious, and satisfying, these are a healthy treat anytime.

MAKES 1 TO 2 SERVINGS

Banana Shake
1½ chilled bananas, sliced
½ cup skim milk
1 tablespoon honey
1 cup crushed ice

Peach Shake
1 cold peach, cut up
½ cup skim milk
Pinch of cinnamon
½ teaspoon sugar
1 cup crushed ice

Tropical Shake
1 banana, sliced
¼ cup strawberries
½ cup pineapple chunks
½ cup pear nectar
1 cup crushed ice

Mixed Berry Shake
⅓ cup fresh raspberries
⅓ cup fresh blueberries
⅓ cup fresh strawberries
1 banana, sliced
1 cup cranberry juice
1 cup crushed ice

Place all ingredients except ice in a blender, and blend until smooth. Pour into glasses filled with crushed ice.

Fruit and Yogurt Smoothies

These easy-to-make smoothies are a healthy way to cool off and relax. They also make a nutritious light breakfast or lunch.

Peaches and Cream Smoothie

3 cups canned peaches in heavy syrup, drained

¾ cup vanilla yogurt

1 cup ice cubes

Blueberry Lemon Smoothie

1 cup blueberries, chilled

1 container (8 ounces) lemon yogurt

1 tablespoon sugar

1 cup ice cubes

Citrus Smoothie

1 cup orange segments, white pith removed

1 can (6 ounces) lime concentrate

1 container (8 ounces) lemon yogurt

1 tablespoon sugar

1 cup ice cubes

Place all the ingredients except ice in a blender and process until smooth. Add the ice cubes and process until crushed.

FRUIT AND NUT SHAKES

Protein, vitamins, and calcium all in one snack—and it tastes great. These shakes are real kid-pleasers. They're so nourishing, you can substitute them for lunch when you're in a hurry.

Chocolate Peanut Butter Banana Shake

⅔ *cup skim milk*

1 large banana, sliced

1 tablespoon reduced-fat smooth peanut butter

1 tablespoon low-fat chocolate syrup

Banana Nut Shake

1 large banana

3 tablespoons pecans

¾ *cup vanilla yogurt*

1 tablespoon honey

Trail Mix Shake

1 banana

½ *cup pitted dates*

½ *cup yogurt*

2 tablespoons almonds

2 tablespoons unsweetened flaked coconut

1 tablespoon honey, or to taste

Combine all the ingredients in the blender and blend until smooth and thick.

Fresh Fruit Spritzers

With a little club soda or seltzer, a simple fresh fruit juice turns into a sparkling party drink. You may need to add some sugar, depending on the sweetness of the fruit. Try some of these at your next get-together, or just treat yourself. If you're in a rush, store-bought juices can be substituted.

MAKES 1 TO 2 SERVINGS

Very Berry Spritzer

1 cup raspberries

1 cup strawberries

2 cups pineapple, cubed

1 cup plain or citrus-flavored seltzer or club soda

Honeydew Mango Pineapple Spritzer

2 cups honeydew, peeled and cubed

1 mango, peeled and pitted

2 cups pineapple, peeled and cubed

1 cup seltzer or club soda

Watermelon Pineapple Lime Spritzer

2 cups watermelon, peeled, seeded, and cubed

2 cups pineapple, peeled and cubed

½ lime, peeled and seeded

1 cup citrus-flavored seltzer or club soda

Pineapple Strawberry Orange Spritzer

2 cups pineapple, peeled and cubed

1 cup strawberries

4 oranges, peeled and seeded

1 lime, peeled and seeded

1 cup Sprite or 7-Up

Peachy Lime Spritzer

3 limes, peeled and seeded

3 peaches, pitted

1 cup citrus-flavored seltzer or club soda

Juice each fruit separately. Combine juices and seltzer or club soda and serve over ice. Add sugar to taste.

Experiment with juicing:

- Juice your favorite fruits and combine with orange juice for a refreshing morning drink.
- Place juice in a blender and add a banana, some yogurt, and honey or maple syrup for a wonderful smoothie.
- Add some light rum, tequila, or your favorite liquor for a fabulous cocktail.

FRESH FRUIT AND VEGETABLE JUICES

You'll need a juicer to prepare these nutritious concoctions. Your taste buds will enjoy the results. Have a glass anytime.

MAKES 1 TO 2 SERVINGS

Carrot Apple Ginger Juice
8 large carrots, peeled
2 apples, seeded
½-inch slice ginger root, peeled

Carrot Pear Pineapple Juice
6 large carrots, peeled
2 pears, seeded and cored
2 cups pineapple, cubed

Apple Raspberry Celery Cucumber Juice
2 cups raspberries
3 apples, seeded and cored
½ cucumber, peeled
1 stalk celery

Pineapple Kiwi Carrot Strawberry Juice
2 cups pineapple, cubed
1 cup strawberries
3 large carrots, peeled
2 kiwis, peeled

Juice each fruit or vegetable separately. Combine the juices. Serve over ice if desired.

Tips for perfect juicing:

• Use the highest-quality fresh produce available.
• Use raw produce—cooking reduces vitamins, minerals, and enzymes.
• Bananas, mangoes, and papayas add flavor and thickness to juices.
• Juice each ingredient separately and then combine, unless otherwise indicated.

MILK SHAKES

Team these delicious drinks with cinnamon graham crackers and jam—or your favorite sandwich or sweet. You can eliminate the fat by substituting fat-free sorbet for the frozen yogurt or ice cream.

MAKES 1 LARGE SHAKE

Low-fat Frozen Yogurt Shake

2 large scoops low-fat vanilla frozen yogurt
1 cup cold skim milk
1 teaspoon vanilla extract
¼ teaspoon ground cinnamon

Chocolate Shake

2 tablespoons chocolate syrup
1 cup cold skim milk
2 large scoops chocolate ice cream

Mocha Shake

1 to 2 tablespoons chocolate syrup
½ cup cold coffee
½ cup skim milk
2 large scoops coffee ice cream

Berry Shake

2 tablespoons raspberry, strawberry, or blueberry syrup
1 cup cold skim milk
½ cup raspberries, strawberries, or blueberries
2 large scoops vanilla, strawberry, or other berry-flavored ice cream
1 tablespoon honey (optional)

Place all the ingredients in a blender. Blend until smooth. Pour into a tall glass and serve immediately.

Sorbet Sodas

Try these light, refreshing takes on the traditional ice cream soda.

Strawberry Sorbet Soda

1 large scoop strawberry sorbet

1 cup strawberry soda or strawberry-
    flavored club soda

1 teaspoon fresh lemon juice (optional)

Raspberry Lemon Sorbet Soda

1 large scoop raspberry sorbet

1 to 2 tablespoons raspberry syrup
    (optional)

½ cup lemonade

½ cup club soda

Tropical Sorbet Soda

1 large scoop mango sorbet

½ cup pineapple juice

1 tablespoon coconut milk

½ cup club soda

Chocolate Raspberry Sorbet Soda

1 large scoop chocolate sorbet

1 to 2 tablespoons raspberry syrup
    (optional)

1 cup raspberry soda or raspberry-
    flavored club soda

Citrus Sorbet Soda

1 large scoop lemon sorbet

½ cup orange juice

½ cup lemon-lime–flavored club soda

Place the sorbet in a tall glass, and pour in the remaining ingredients. Serve immediately with a tall spoon.

Try these fabulous ice cream soda combinations:
- Chocolate syrup, vanilla ice cream, and club soda
- Strawberry syrup, strawberry ice cream, and ginger ale
- Chocolate syrup, coffee ice cream, and club soda
- Chocolate syrup, chocolate ice cream, and club soda
- Chocolate syrup, mint ice cream, and club soda
- Vanilla ice cream and root beer soda
- Your favorite fruit syrup, vanilla ice cream, and club soda

Or for an interesting variation, combine your favorite sorbet or ice cream and 1 to 2 tablespoons of your favorite syrup. Then fill the glass with a carbonated beverage. Garnish with fresh mint, a twist of lemon or lime, fresh fruit, or chocolate shavings.

Index

A

aïoli, garlic, 36
almonds:
  in granola, 49
  toasted, baked Brie stuffed
    with strawberry
    preserves and, 45
apple(s):
  baked, with dried cranberries
    and granola, 136
  chicken, and cheddar pizza,
    70–71
  cider, hot, 160
  raspberry celery cucumber
    juice, 170
  romaine burritos with blue
    cheese, chicken, pecans
    and, 63
apricot:
  dipping sauce, sesame pecan
    chicken tenders with,
    116
  preserves, Camembert with
    pecans, dried
    cranberries and, 44

preserves in sweet and spicy
    dipping sauce, 116
artichoke(s):
  and mushrooms, marinated,
    37
  pesto, and olive pizza, 68–69
Asian dipping sauce, creamy,
    112

B

bacon:
  in BLT quesadillas, 78–79
  and blue cheese toasts, 41
  fontina, and sun-dried
    tomato sandwich,
    grilled, 57
  mayonnaise, 59
  and shrimp filling, 108
  in stuffed mushrooms, 103
  in stuffed potato skins, 72–73
  -wrapped shrimp with soy
    dipping sauce, 114
bagel chips, 23
banana:
  chip muffins, 128

nut shake, 167
shake, 165
barbecue chicken pizza, 70–71
bars:
  chocolate cookie, 146
  date and nut, 129
basil:
  goat cheese log with sun-
    dried tomatoes and, 42
  pesto dip, 34
  pesto wedges, 34
bean:
  black, dip, 27
  and cheese quesadillas, 78–79
beef:
  in cocktail meatballs, 113
  open-faced roast, 55
  in Tex-Mex filling, 108
  in Tex-Mex pizza, 70–71
berry:
  dip, 150
  lemonade, 161
  shake, 171
  shake, mixed, 165
  spritzer, very, 168
black bean dip, 27

blondies, hazelnut, 130
BLT quesadillas, 78–79
blueberry lemon smoothie, 166
blue cheese:
    and bacon toasts, 41
    romaine burritos with
        chicken, apples, pecans
        and, 63
bread, broccoli and cheese, 64
breadsticks with prosciutto and
    Robiola, 89
Brie:
    and mango quesadillas,
        78–79
    stuffed, 43
    stuffed with strawberry
        preserves and toasted
        almonds, baked, 45
broccoli and cheese bread, 64
bruschetta, tomato, 86
budget, 2, 7
burritos, romaine, with blue
    cheese, chicken, apples,
    and pecans, 63

C

café:
    au lait, 154
    latte, 157
    mocha, 154
    con panna, 155
    vanilla, 155
California:
    grilled sandwich, 58
    nachos, 80–81

Camembert with apricot
    preserves, pecans, and
    dried cranberries, 44
cappuccino, 156
caramel munch, 48
carrot:
    apple ginger juice, 170
    fresh vegetables stuffed with
        green onions, radish, and
        carrot cream cheese, 96
    pear pineapple juice, 170
cereal cookies, 124
cheddar, chicken, and apple
    pizza, 70–71
cheese:
    in barbecue chicken pizza,
        70–71
    and bean quesadillas, 78–79
    in berry dip, 150
    and broccoli bread, 64
    in Buffalo chicken wings, 74
    in California grilled
        sandwich, 58
    in California nachos, 80–81
    in fried ravioli, 105
    fruit and nut salsa with
        Roquefort, 33
    and garlic twists, 25
    in Greek pizza, 70–71
    in icing, 132
    in Italian-style nachos, 80–81
    in light mini cheesecakes,
        133
    in Mexican pizza, 71
    nachos, 80–81
    in nachos grandes, 80–81

in pesto, olive, and artichoke
    pizza, 68–69
in pizza filling, 107
in pizza muffins, 65
in pretzel rolls, 60
quesadillas, 78–79
quesadillas, spicy, 78–79
raspberry filling, 108
in salad pizza, 70–71
in smoked salmon pizza,
    68–69
in smoked salmon spread,
    109
spinach and Feta puffs,
    104
in spinach Florentine filling,
    107
in stuffed eggplant, 101
in stuffed mushrooms, 103
in stuffed potato skins, 72–73
in sun-dried tomato
    quesadillas, 78–79
in Tex-Mex filling, 108
in Tex-Mex hot dogs, 56
in Tex-Mex pizza, 70–71
in tomato garlic pizza, 71
and tomato pizza, 68–69
in tuna melt muffins, 65
in white pizza, 71
see also specific cheeses
cheesecakes, light mini, 133
chicken:
    apple, and cheddar pizza,
        70–71
    barbecue, pizza, 70–71
    liver pâté, 97

romaine burritos with blue cheese, apples, pecans and, 63

satay, 32

in sausage in blankets, 110

tenders, sesame pecan, with apricot dipping sauce, 116

in Tex-Mex pizza, 70–71

wings, Buffalo, 74

chips:

bagel, 23

Mexican, 22

pita, 22

savory, 22

sweet, 22

chocolate:

in banana chip muffins, 128

in café mocha, 154

in candy shop cookies, 120

in coffee egg cream, 162

cookie bars, 146

in hazelnut blondies, 130

hazelnut thins, 123

hot, 159

in ice cream cookiewiches, 137

in individual black-and-white ice cream pies, 138–139

in low-fat frozen cookie pudding, 140

in mochaccino, 156

in mocha latte, 157

in mocha shake, 171

in ol'-fashioned egg cream, 162

peanut butter banana shake, 167

peanut butter candy squares, 143

raspberry sorbet soda, 172

sauce, 151

shake, 171

truffles with Kahlúa and pecans, 144

white, –covered dried fruit, 149

white, raisin nut bark, 148

yogurt pops, low-fat, 141

cider, hot apple, 160

citrus:

smoothie, 166

sorbet soda, 172

clam dip loaf, baked, 35

cobbler, easy fruit, 135

cocktail:

meatballs, 113

sandwiches, ham and Swiss, 87

coffee:

egg cream, 162

smoothie, 158

smoothies, frozen, 158

specialties, brewed, 154–155

cold hors d'oeuvre party, 14

cookie(s):

bars, chocolate, 146

candy shop, 120

cereal, 124

lemon pignoli crisps, 121

nutty thumbprint, 122

pudding, low-fat frozen, 140

cookiewiches, ice cream, 137

crab (meat):

cakes, mini, 115

fritters, 111

vegetable filling, cherry tomatoes with, 90

cranberry(ies):

baked apples with granola and dried, 136

Camembert with apricot preserves, pecans, and dried, 44

dried, in granola, 49

orange scones, 126–127

sauce in cocktail meatballs, 113

turkey rollwich, 54–55

cream cheese:

and cucumber sandwiches, 66–67

fresh vegetables stuffed with green onions, radish, and carrot, 96

tomato, and red onion muffins, 65

crisps:

lemon pignoli, 121

tortilla, 24

crostini topped with sun-dried tomato and roasted red pepper pesto and goat cheese, 84

cucumber:

and cream cheese sandwiches, 66–67

strawberry banana colada, 164

strawberry daiquiri, 164

strawberry sorbet soda, 172

trail mix shake, 167

tropical shake, 165

tropical sorbet soda, 172

very berry spritzer, 168

watermelon pineapple lime spritzer, 168

E

egg cream, good ol'-fashioned, 162

eggplant, stuffed, 101

eggs:

    chopped, mushrooms, and onions on black bread, 61

    deviled, with sun-dried tomato and roasted pepper pesto, 93

    in vegetable frittata on baguette, 62

endive leaves, dilled shrimp salad on, 94

English muffins, gourmet, 65

espresso romano, 156

F

Feta and spinach puffs, 104

finger sandwiches, 66–67

focaccia in a snap, 88

fontina, sun-dried tomato, and bacon sandwich, grilled, 57

freezer and pantry, ready-to-munch, 17–19

frittata, vegetable, on a baguette, 62

fritters, crab, 111

fruit:

    cobbler, easy, 135

    and nut salsa with Roquefort, 33

    and nut shakes, 167

    shakes, frozen, 165

    split, tropical, 142

    spritzers, fresh, 168–169

    and vegetable juices, fresh, 170

    white chocolate–covered dried, 149

    and yogurt smoothies, 166

G

garlic:

    aïoli, 36

    and cheese twists, 25

    and herb tomatoes, 98

    knots, 26

    in marinated niçoise olives, 38

    and roasted pepper dip, tricolor tortellini skewers with, 99

    tomato pizza, 71

    in white pizza, 71

gingerbread, 131

glazed walnuts, 51

goat cheese:

    crostini topped with sun-dried tomato and roasted pepper pesto and, 84

    log with sun-dried tomatoes and basil, 42

    marinated, with crumb crust, 46

    and sun-dried tomato muffins, 65

granola, 49

    baked apples with dried cranberries and, 136

Greek pizza, 70–71

green sauce, 29

guests, 1–2

H

ham and Swiss cocktail sandwiches, 87

hazelnut:

    blondies, 130

    chocolate thins, 123

    egg cream, 162

    espresso smoothie, 158

herb and garlic tomatoes, 98

honeydew mango pineapple spritzer, 168

honey mustard and turkey sandwiches, 66–67

horseradish:

    tuna on cucumber rounds, 92

    yogurt sauce, 77

hot chocolate, 159
hot dogs, Tex-Mex, 56

I

ice cream:
    cookiewiches, 137
    pies, individual black-and-
        white, 138–139
iced tea, flavored, 163
icing, 132
island paradise, 164
Italian-style nachos, 80–81

J

juices, fresh fruit and vegetable,
    170

K

Kahlúa, chocolate truffles with
    pecans and, 144

L

lemon:
    limeade, 161
    pignoli crisps, 121
lemonade, 161
low-fat:
    chocolate yogurt pops,
        141
    frozen cookie pudding, 140
    frozen yogurt shake, 171

M

macadamia nuts, orange, 50
mango:
    and Brie quesadillas, 78–79
    salsa, spicy, 30
mayonnaise, bacon, 59
meatballs, cocktail, 113
menus, 4–16
    cheese with preserves, jams,
        and chutneys, 12
    cocktail party tidbits, 5
    coffee and . . . , 15
    cold hors d'oeuvre party,
        14
    creating of, 4
    dessert bar, 16
    elegant on a budget, 7
    elegant springtime treat,
        14
    holiday nibbles, 6
    hot hors d'oeuvre party,
        13
    midnight munchies, 11
    poolside hors d'oeuvres, 8
    pub food, 10
    summer hors d'oeuvres in
        the garden, 15
    Super Bowl snacks, 10
    a taste of Italy, 9
    teatime, 16
    Tex-Mex munchies, 8
    you can't go wrong, 7
Mexican:
    chips, 22
    pizza, 71

milk shakes, 171
mocha:
    latte, 157
    shake, 171
mochaccino, 156
mozzarella and prosciutto
        stuffing, plum tomatoes
        with, 100
muffins:
    banana chip, 128
    cream cheese, tomato, and
        red onion, 65
    goat cheese and sun-dried
        tomato, 65
    pizza, 65
    tuna melt, 65
mushrooms:
    and artichokes, marinated,
        37
    chopped eggs, and onions on
        black bread, 61
    stuffed, 103
    in vegetable frittata on
        baguette, 62
mustard, honey, and turkey
        sandwiches, 66–67

N

nachos, 80–81
    grandes, 80–81
niçoise olives, marinated,
    38
nut:
    bark, white chocolate raisin,
        148

and date bars, 129
and fruit salsa with
Roquefort, 33
and fruit shakes, 167
raisin twists, 125
nutty thumbprint cookies,
122

O

occasions and guests, 1–2
olivada, black, 39
olive(s):
 in Greek pizza, 70–71
 niçoise, marinated, 38
 pesto, and artichoke pizza,
 68–69
 in puttanesca focaccia,
 88
onion(s):
 chopped eggs, and
 mushrooms on black
 bread, 61
 focaccia, 88
 fresh vegetables stuffed
 with green onion,
 radish, and carrot
 cream cheese, 96
 muffins, cream cheese,
 tomato, and red, 65
 rings, crispy, with spicy
 dipping sauce, 75
orange:
 cranberry scones,126–127
 macadamia nuts, 50
oreganata, scallops, 102

P

pancakes, potato, 117
pantry and freezer, ready–to-
munch, 17–19
pâté, chicken liver, 97
peach(es):
 and cream smoothie,
 166
 shake, 165
peachy lime spritzer, 168
peanut:
 brittle, double, 147
 butter chocolate candy
 squares, 143
 sauce, Thai, 32
 in Southwestern mix, 47
pecan(s):
 Camembert with apricot
 preserves, dried
 cranberries and, 44
 chocolate truffles with
 Kahlúa and, 144
 in granola, 49
 romaine burritos with blue
 cheese, chicken, apples,
 and, 63
 sesame chicken tenders with
 apricot dipping sauce,
 116
pepper, roasted:
 focaccia, 88
 and garlic dip, tricolor
 tortellini with, 99
 and sun-dried tomato pesto,
 85

and sun-dried tomato pesto,
 crostini topped with
 goat cheese and, 84
and sun-dried tomato pesto,
 deviled eggs with, 93
in zucchini rolls, 91
pesto:
 cream and sun-dried tomato
 sandwiches, 66–67
 dip, basil, 34
 olive, and artichoke pizza,
 68–69
 sun-dried tomato and
 roasted pepper, 85
 sun-dried tomato and roasted
 pepper, crostini topped
 with goat cheese and, 84
 sun-dried tomato and
 roasted pepper, deviled
 eggs with, 93
 wedges, basil, 34
pignoli lemon crisps, 121
piña colada, 164
pineapple:
 kiwi carrot strawberry juice,
 170
 strawberry orange spritzer,
 168
 in tropical fruit split, 142
pita:
 chips, 22
 pizza, 71
pizza(s):
 filling, 107
 muffins, 65
 personal, 68–69